THE BIG BUSINESS OF
SAVING THE WORLD

THE BIG BUSINESS OF SAVING THE WORLD

JORDAN CYNEWSKI

NEW DEGREE PRESS

THE BIG BUSINESS OF SAVING THE WORLD

ISBN   978-1-64137-222-0   *Paperback*

         978-1-64137-223-7   *Ebook*

For my mother, Althea, who taught me to love reading,
writing, and learning;
for my father, Steven, who taught me how to be a good man;
and for my brother, Jared, who taught me everything in between.

Without you, this book would not exist, and I would not be the
person I am today. I love you all.

CONTENTS

PART I

THE RISE OF THE INTERNATIONAL CORPORATION

INTRODUCTION

———

LIQUID GOLD

Coffee. If you're anything like me, you can't go a day without this simple concoction. I'm drinking coffee as I write this, and you may very well be drinking some as you read this. America runs on it. The world runs on it. Just beans and water—that's all.

According to one apocryphal tale, the stimulating quality of coffee beans was first discovered in the eighth century by an Ethiopian goat herder named Kaldi, who observed that his flock became hyperactive after consuming the leaves of the plant. After trying it himself, Kaldi brought the plants to a nearby monastery to be examined by a monk. The monk, disapproving of this plant's consumption, tossed it into a fire.

From the flames emerged a tantalizing aroma that attracted the interest of the other monks in the monastery. They supposedly removed the roasted beans from the fire, ground them, and combined them with hot water to produce the first ever cup of coffee.[1]

It's unlikely that dollar signs appeared in Kaldi's eyes when he looked upon his new discovery, but more entrepreneurial individuals certainly had them in the centuries that followed. But through centuries of globalization, what was once straightforward has become incredibly complex. Beginning in the Middle Ages, coffee made its way out of its native Ethiopia, brought to Yemen by Somali traders and gradually spreading across the world through Arabia.

As international trade has expanded and developed over the years, it has also become increasingly complex. Especially in recent years, technology has improved at an unprecedented rate, enabling unforeseen progress in international communication and transportation. For businesses, it has never been easier to optimize efficiency by obtaining resources where they are plentiful, manufacturing products where labor is

---

1   Bennett Alan Weinberg, *The World Of Caffeine: The Science And Culture Of The World's Most Popular Drug* (New York: Routledge, 2002), https://books.google.com/books?id=Qyz5CnOaH9oC&pg=PA3&dq=coffee+goat+ethiopia+Kaldi&lr=&ei=paxHStuDJ4Xu-zATj97hf#v=onepage&q=coffee goat ethiopia Kaldi&f=false, 3-4.

cheap, and selling goods where people can afford to pay the most for them. Thus, the global supply chain was born.

In the twenty-first century, coffee no longer seems so simple. After crude oil, coffee is the second most sought-after commodity in the world, with a global industry valued at over $100 billion.[2] *Business Insider* estimates that coffee exporting alone is a $20 billion industry and growing.[3]

Rising demand for coffee has caused it to play a major role in the lives of ever more people in a wide array of countries around the planet. Today, some 25 million people worldwide earn their living on coffee farms.[4] But the statistics for production and consumption show a stark contrast. Over 90 percent of global coffee production occurs in developing countries, while it is mostly consumed in developed countries.[5]

This sheer physical distance between the producer and the consumer makes full transparency difficult to achieve. After

---

2 Eric Goldschein, "11 Incredible Facts About The Global Coffee Industry," *Business Insider*, https://www.businessinsider.com/facts-about-the-coffee-industry-2011-11.

3 Ibid.

4 Ibid.

5 Stefano Ponte, "The 'Latte Revolution'? Regulation, Markets And Consumption In The Global Coffee Chain," *World Development*, vol. 30, no. 7, July 2002, https://www.semanticscholar.org/paper/The-'Latte-Revolution'-Regulation,-Markets-and-in-Ponte/7b2f-9274b27c0babc6148434bdbd8a2b62a7b5da, 1199.

all, a company cannot easily disclose every fact of every step of every product's journey through a complex global supply chain. In many cases, the company has trouble even discerning these facts for itself.

A lack of transparency breeds a lack of knowledge, and a lack of knowledge is dangerous. It can open the door to any manner of wrongdoing anywhere along the global supply chain. A company might abuse its workers, for example, or wreak environmental havoc far from the eyes of its consumers.

All of a sudden, that coffee you hold in your hands entails substantial, far-reaching ethical considerations. *Business Insider* estimates that over 500 billion cups of coffee are consumed every year,[6] although some scholars believe that global coffee consumption may in fact exceed 800 billion cups annually.[7] Still, a report by Conservation International projected that increasing demand will force the coffee industry to expand production by as much as three times by 2050,[8] a concerning prognosis given that most of the unused land suitable for coffee production is currently covered by

---

6   Goldschein, "The Global Coffee Industry."

7   Ibid.

8   "Future Demand And Climate Change Could Make Coffee A Driver Of Deforestation," *Conservation International*, 2016, https://www.conservation.org/NewsRoom/pressreleases/Pages/Future-Demand-and-Climate-Change-Could-Make-Coffee-a-Driver-of-Deforestation-.aspx.

rainforest. Ohio State University's Amanda Varcho describes, "There are two types of coffee plants, those that grow in sun and those that grow in shade. The sun grown coffee plant has been tailored to produce nearly three times as much coffee as the shade version. Increased production of sun grown coffee plants results in greater loss of rainforest."[9] Growing demand will force coffee companies, constantly competing with each other in the global marketplace, to optimize their production through the use of sun-grown plants, necessitating increased deforestation.

The question then arises: do international corporations have some *social* responsibility apart from simply turning a profit?

In order to cater to a growing number of consumers demanding greater moral accountability in business, more and more companies are engaging in corporate social responsibility (CSR) programs, challenging themselves to go beyond their financial obligations and help find solutions to social problems in their local communities.

---

9   Clark, Kylienne, Travis Shaul, Brian H. Lower, and Amanda L. Varcho, "2.2 A Bitter Brew- Coffee Production, Deforestation, Soil Erosion And Water Contamination," 2015, *Ohiostate.Pressbooks. Pub.*, https://ohiostate.pressbooks.pub/sciencebites/chapter/a-bitter-brew-coffee-production-deforestation-soil-erosion-and-water-contamination/.

One common metric for CSR in agricultural industries like coffee is whether a third-party nonprofit organization has inspected the process of production and verified it as Fair Trade Certified™. This label indicates that a business satisfies certain social standards set by the certifying institution, such as adequately compensating workers and minimizing environmental damage.

But international CSR is not so simple. Thanks to the growing intricacy of global supply chains, a mere label can no longer sufficiently determine whether a business is wholly moral or immoral.

"Coffee-producing companies claim 90% of their coffee comes from fair trade locations," explains Mac McGary, president of the Sweetbridge Blockchain Alliance. "But you only survey every five to 10 years, and the local government knows you're coming, so they're complicit in hiding the children and staging the process so that they're compliant because they don't want to lose business."[10]

In an effort to retain contracts with foreign corporations, governments of developing countries permit unethical business practices such as child labor on coffee farms—meaning that struggling farmers in these countries often have no

---

10   "Sweetbridge," 2019, https://sweetbridge.com/platform/.

choice but to endure inhumane working conditions to get by financially.

Sweetbridge uses technological innovation to tackle international CSR dilemmas at their source: the lack of transparency in global supply chains. Using blockchain, the same kind of technology that powers cryptocurrencies like bitcoin, Sweetbridge forgoes the ineffective regular audits required for fair trade certifications. Instead, as the company website explains, it is "building real-time auditing with code that automatically tracks transactions and can be built for automatic compliance with regulations. This allows [Sweetbridge] to lower risk and create a system where everyone can liberate the value they own, saving time and freeing up money."[11] Put differently, they are applying new technology in a socially responsible manner to defend the rights of workers in developing countries while also increasing transparency and decreasing transactions costs for businesses.

In McGary's words, "We don't want brands to disengage from whole regions because of a few bad actors, so how do we reward bad actors for good behavior? If we can validate with electronic records [through blockchain], then they would then be eligible to get supply chain financing at a lower cost.

---

11   Ibid.

We found you could incentivize people to do the right thing at the local level by giving them access to capital."[9]

But there are still other, simpler ways your coffee can be socially responsible, such as self-imposed regulation. Starbucks, for example, runs a highly successful Coffee and Farmer Equity (CAFE) program. At its core, CAFE is a set of purchasing guidelines Starbucks uses to ensure all of its coffee meets a minimum standard of quality, is sustainably grown, and can be traced through payment records back to fairly compensated farmers who work in humane conditions.[12]

Note that each aspect of this CSR initiative relates directly to the central mission and daily operations of the company. Starbucks could instead devote its CSR efforts to raising money for heart disease research and patient support, but then its social purpose would be entirely distinct from its financial purpose. As finances are the lifeline and engine of any business, it makes sense for the company to tie its social objectives to its financial ones if the former are ever to be achieved.

As you can see, there's more to your cup of coffee than meets the eye. Such is the case for any good or service you

---

12 "Coffee," Starbucks Coffee Company, 2014, https://www.starbucks.ie/responsibility/sourcing/coffee.

purchase from any international company. From the food you eat and the clothes you wear to the electronics you use and the investments you make, wherever you look, the ever-growing web of global supply and demand comes tangled with ethical quandaries affecting countless people in countless places.

WHY I WROTE THIS BOOK

I intend to demonstrate that global business has not only the capability but the imperative to do well financially by doing good socially.

Critics of international CSR might suggest that self-interested corporations can never truly maintain a set of social values. Rather, they use CSR as a clever marketing tool to appear conscientious in the eyes of the public and attract customers despite having no genuine commitment to resolving social problems.

This concern is valid, and many companies do in fact lack authenticity in their CSR commitments. One example of CSR inauthenticity is the trend of "greenwashing," or the act of misleading customers to believe a company is more environmentally conscious than it truly is. Even some of the world's largest polluters such as ExxonMobil regularly engage in deceptive tactics like this. Clearly, the current model of international CSR must be modernized.

I stumbled across this topic in an attempt to reconcile my own desires to do good for the world and simultaneously achieve personal financial success.

The two defining features of the modern world are globalization and the market. That is the world my generation has grown up in, and this book is my attempt to make some sense of it. If you live in any developed society, international corporations play an astronomical role in your life. If you don't believe me, just look around you and consider every object in the room. Unless you deliberately live an ultra-sustainable lifestyle, it's likely that almost every object you see had something to do with international business, whether related to investment, resource extraction, manufacturing, or transportation. And every international business you interact with touches countless other lives in countries across the world.

I became fascinated with the complex ethical dilemmas that arise as a result of global supply chains and decided to research the topic in depth. I spent months gathering information and interviewing a number of experts in the field, including business executives, professors, nonprofit leaders, and investors. I learned all I could about the greatest challenges facing international CSR and evaluated different approaches to these challenges. The final result was this book.

Today's consumers no longer believe in the old model of CSR. With unparalleled access to information through the internet and the ability to coordinate efforts through social media, consumers are better suited than ever before to holding corporations accountable. According to recent data, this recent trend of consumer empowerment does not apply exclusively to millennials or Gen X—even Baby Boomers have begun to more closely consider corporate ethics when making purchasing decisions in recent years.[13]

We now place a great value on authenticity; as Sweetbridge Blockchain Alliance, Starbucks, and many more have already demonstrated, the key to authenticity lies in the supply chain.

I contend that the global supply chain should become the new framework for businesses and their stakeholders to think about CSR. This framework will consist of the following three key points:

---

13   Anjali Lai, "Millennials Call For Values-Driven Companies, But They're Not The Only Ones Interested," Forbes (Forbes Magazine, May 23, 2018), https://www.forbes.com/sites/forrester/2018/05/23/millennials-call-for-values-driven-companies-but-theyre-not-the-only-ones-interested/#7cb740a55464.

Recognizing and resolving problems along the supply chain.

- Maintaining genuine, long-term social commitments.
- Articulating a coherent narrative about the supply chain and how the business is investing in it.

My hope is that the information contained in this book will prove useful to executives at large companies, of course, but also to younger workers looking for impactful and lucrative careers, investors seeking substantial returns through ethical means, and regular people who want to make better informed decisions with their money. Whoever you are, you are certain to benefit from knowing the playbook for the next decade of international CSR.

Just as corporations can contribute to the world's problems or the solutions to those problems, so too can individuals. As we will see later on, many aspects of CSR today are, in a sense, broken. I hope that by educating more people on the subject, this book can be part of the solution for a malfunctioning system.

CHAPTER 1

THE CURRENT STATE OF CSR IN A GLOBALIZED WORLD

Accounts of corporate wrongdoing appear to have multiplied in today's increasingly international economy. Ride-sharing app Uber, which operates in over 60 countries across the world, has been plagued by accusations of fostering a culture of sexual harassment, using "Greyball" software to evade government authorities in localities across the planet where the company was operating illegally, and failing to protect the information of 57 million users whose data was stolen by hackers in 2017.[14] Relatively new major players

---

14 Lucinda Shen, "The 10 Biggest Business Scandals of 2017," Fortune, December 31, 2017, http://fortune.com/2017/12/31/

in the global market, including internet giants like Facebook, Twitter, and Google's parent company, Alphabet, have also recently become the subject of corporate wrongdoing. These titans of tech have all come under fire for allegedly corrupting U.S. democracy by selling political advertisements to entities linked with the Russian government and luring users in by manipulating their addictive tendencies only to sell their information to private third parties.[15]

Some of these transgressions even appear to be directly linked to the international nature of these companies. For example, in 2010, 18 employees of the Taiwanese company Foxconn, a major tech manufacturer, leapt from the roof of their Shenzhen factory in protest of their abominable working conditions. In 2012 alone, Foxconn openly admitted that it had illegally employed children, 150 of its employees threatened to commit mass suicide, 2,000 more participated in a riot against the security forces at their worker dormitories, and an audit of the company by the Fair Labor Association found workers subjected to 34-hour stretches of overtime. Foxconn continues to supply products for some of the world's largest companies, including Apple, Sony, HP, and Nintendo, meaning that most Americans own at least

---

biggest-corporate-scandals-misconduct-2017-pr/.

15 Shen, "Are Facebook, Google, Twitter Manipulating Users? Washington Wants to Know," Fortune, December 27, 2017, http://fortune.com/2017/12/27/facebook-google-twitter-addiction/.

one product manufactured under these heinous global supply chain abuses.

But these issues aren't exclusive to the tech industry. According to a recent report from the United Kingdom's Carbon Disclosure Project, over 70 percent of worldwide greenhouse gas emissions in the last three decades were produced by just 100 massive companies, mostly in the energy industry.[16] In 2014, a report by the Fair Labor Association found that Nestle had employed child laborers to do the same dangerous jobs as adult workers.[17] More recently, in 2017, an NGO report found that the food industry titan had illegally grown much of its cocoa in protected lands in the Ivory Coast, having deforested over 90 percent of the land in these areas.[18] In 2017, the consumer credit reporting agency Equifax collected the personal information of nearly half of the U.S. population and illegally sold it to other entities.[19] Across an array of

---

16 Paul Griffin, "CDP Carbon Majors Report 2017," *The Carbon Majors Database*, https://b8f65cb373b1b7b15feb-c70d8ead-6ced550b4d987d7c03fcdd1d.ssl.cf3.rackcdn.com/cms/reports/documents/000/002/327/original/Carbon-Majors-Report-2017.pdf?1499691240

17 "2014 Assessments of Shared Hazelnut Supply Chain In Turkey: Nestlé, Balsu, and Olam," fairlabor.org (Fair Labor Association, May 4, 2015), http://www.fairlabor.org/2014-hazelnuts-independent-external-assessments.

18 Etelle Higonnet, Marisa Bellantonio, and Glenn Hurowitz, "Chocolate's Dark Secret: How The Cocoa Industry Destroys National Parks," *Mightyearth.Org*, 2017, http://www.mightyearth.org/wp-content/uploads/2017/09/chocolates_dark_secret_english_web.pdf.

19 Hamza Shaban, "Equifax CEO Richard Smith Steps down amid Hacking Scandal," The Washington Post (WP Company,

vastly different industries, multinational companies have wrought catastrophes in recent years, harming children, the environment, and millions of unsuspecting, innocent people all at once.

So it's easy to see why so many people have become skeptical of multinational corporations. People have mobilized against corporatism, globalization, and even capitalism itself. According to figures from Gallup, 68 percent of Americans aged 18–29 viewed capitalism favorably in 2010, the year before the Occupy Wall Street movement began. In less than a decade, that number dropped by over 20 percent. According to Gallup's most recent polling in 2018, less than half of Americans aged 18–29 expressed a positive view of capitalism.[20]

But the scale of corporate misdeeds does not necessarily grow in proportion to the size of corporations themselves. In fact, the market punishes the businesses responsible for these corporate misdeeds and rewards businesses that create social good. For example, following the news of Uber's series of irresponsible missteps, the company's market share

September 26, 2017), https://www.washingtonpost.com/news/the-switch/wp/2017/09/26/equifax-ceo-retires-following-massive-data-breach/?utm_term=.4f8e2077202b.

20 Frank Newport, "Democrats More Positive About Socialism Than Capitalism," Gallup.com (Gallup, August 13, 2018), https://news.gallup.com/poll/240725/democrats-positive-socialism-capitalism.aspx.

dropped 10 percent last year, its valuation plummeted from $68 billion to $48 billion, and CEO Travis Kalanick was fired.[21] The important fact many people miss is that the larger the business, the more visibility its transgressions (as well as its charitable acts) receive. As has been the case with Uber, dissatisfied stakeholders in morally reprehensible firms will take their business elsewhere. Meanwhile, a business widely known for its service as a global citizen and steward for humanity is likely to attract more stakeholders who approve of its conscientiousness and want to help further its mission.

This, then, raises the question of why so many companies today still seem to engage in irresponsible practices. Part of the answer is simply that sometimes things just seem worse than they really are. For example, many people were outraged when the Economic Policy Institute released the results of a study that found that, on average, U.S. CEOs bring in 271 times the salary of the lowest paid employee at their company.[22] While this ostensibly reinforces the popular image of pervasive corporate greed, it actually represents the latest data point in a steady decline in wage

---

21 Shen, "The 10 Biggest Business Scandals of 2017."
22 Lawrence Mishel and Jessica Schieder, "CEO Pay Remains High-Relative to the Pay of Typical Workers and High Wage Earners," Economic Policy Institute (EPI, July 20, 2017), https://www.epi.org/publication/ceo-pay-remains-high-relative-to-the-pay-of-typical-workers-and-high-wage-earners/.

disparity since the all-time high in 2000, when the salaries of CEOs were 376 times that of their employees.[23] Although the situation seems to be worsening, this inequality has in fact decreased by over 25 percent over the course of the twenty-first century so far.

But the fact remains that many corporations still commit grave misdeeds. They believe they can get away with their wrongdoing or that any risk of experiencing negative consequences is worth the benefit. In the chapters that follow, I will devote a great deal of attention to how this thought process is misguided. Just because porations can and sometimes do represent a source of misery for selfish gain does not mean they should.

Much of the time, in fact, we shall see that it is not only in the best interest of society as a whole but also of the corporation itself to uphold genuine social commitments. Aside from the direct social benefits, an effective CSR program can improve a company's public image; draw in positive media coverage; bolster employee engagement, creativity, growth, and retention; and attract and retain investors and business partners. Nevertheless, the reputation of international businesses has suffered in recent years thanks

---

23   Ibid.

to the kinds of misdeeds mentioned at the beginning of this chapter.

Some may even go so far as to blame technological globalization. It is easy to draw conclusions about the relationship between the unethical behavior of multinational corporations and the technological revolution of the last few decades that has made our world increasingly international. Technology facilitates the expansion of corporations abroad by enabling more efficient information processing, transportation, and communication across borders. More international companies means more opportunity for international corporate irresponsibility. Recent technological developments have also opened possibilities for whole new forms of irresponsibility, such as the illegal, nonconsensual harvesting of millions of people's personal data in the Facebook-Cambridge Analytica scandal of the past few years. Technology enabled corporate globalization and, with it, greater international corporate wrongdoing.

Because many people have come to perceive globalization as a problem rather than a solution, movements in countries across the world have begun to retreat from the global arena, turning instead toward nationalism. However, this trend only presents an additional challenge for corporations trying to work toward a global good as it discourages people from backing their international missions and instead encourages them to look inward rather than outward, isolating their communities. Perception, whether accurate or not, matters. A challenge for corporate social responsibility in the modern world, therefore, is the need to devise strategies to overcome this insular mindset.

An equally important yet often overlooked challenge associated with international corporate social responsibility is its underlying subjectivity. Regardless of your personal views on cultural relativism, you must act within the social norms of the country or countries where you do business. Drastic differences in morality across various regions of the world can complicate things for businesses operating in multiple countries simply because what one culture accepts as ethical behavior may be unanimously considered depraved elsewhere.

Elzbieta Krzanowski, a consultant with years of experience as an international development professional, contends that the root of international corporate social responsibility lies in the transfer of knowledge. "I have always thought that sharing our Western know-how is very important as long as we don't insist or put pressure on others to do it our way just because that's how we do it here in this country," she said. "We need to concentrate on knowledge and skill development, which changes mindsets and the way people think and conduct themselves and the work that they do."

International CSR should not be about imposing the values of one culture onto another. Instead, it should be about sharing knowledge, creating wealth, and spreading empowerment.

"We need to let them learn for the benefit of their countries and our world," Elizabeth added. "We all want to live in a better educated, more peaceful, better functioning world, and education is the most important part of that. But we can't pretend we know best because we don't. There are cultural, structural, and religious differences, so we can't insist on anything. We can only present what we know and hope that those we address will learn from it and adapt to better themselves and to better the world."

The focus, then, should be on skill-building rather than democracy-building. Corporations must therefore carefully tread the line between modernizing societies and Westernizing them.

After all, much of what complicates all international corporate activities, including CSR, is that every culture does business differently. "Prior to the expansion of international trade in the nineteenth and twentieth centuries, most commerce was local and followed traditional norms and ethical standards," explained professor Guillermo C. Jimenez and Elizabeth Pulos, senior manager of compliance administration at Worldwide Responsible Accredited Production.

"With the expansion of international trade, however, businesses began to operate across cultural and linguistic boundaries. Misunderstandings and transgressions, both intended and unintended, became commonplace."[24]

The obstacles to cross-cultural interaction they describe also become issues of CSR on the international scale, largely because "specific business activities that are considered acceptable in some societies may be considered taboo in others," Jimenez and Pulos elaborated. "Thus, the American practice of lobbying legislators and governmental agencies would be considered an illegal form of buying influence in many other countries. In some societies, gift giving to chiefs, elders, or religious leaders is considered not only acceptable and appropriate, but even a mandatory traditional expression of respect and obligation."[25] What one country deems ethical may be regarded as unethical elsewhere, therefore it is crucial for corporations to tailor their CSR endeavors not just to one society's idea of social progress but to a broader, more global notion of objective progress.

---

24 Guillermo C. Jimenez and Elizabeth Pulos, "Corruption In International Business," *Good Corporation, Bad Corporation: Corporate Social Responsibility In The Global Economy*, 2017, https://milnepublishing.geneseo.edu/good-corporation-bad-corporation/chapter/10-corruption-in-international-business/.
25 Ibid.

Globalization and capitalism are, admittedly, imperfect. Although each is often demonized in its own right, I hope to prove in the remaining chapters of this book that international corporations can and must be a force for global good.

CHAPTER 2

IDEOLOGY AND THE
GLOBAL SUPPLY CHAIN

———

NATIONALISTS AND GLOBALISTS: TWO VISIONS FOR THE WORLD ECONOMY

Recent decades of globalization have brought the world to a crossroads in more ways than one. Politically, economically, and socially, the world today is more interconnected than it ever has been, but many worry the recent developments that have ostensibly brought disparate people closer together may also drive them apart. This book is meant to neither endorse nor reject any particular political ideology, but given the relevance of changing economic policies to the present state of international corporate social responsibility, some background knowledge of the topic is necessary.

At the end of the last millennium, globalism, an ideology supporting globalization, emerged as the dominant viewpoint shaping international affairs.

In the twenty-first century, the world has witnessed a resurgence of economic nationalism, a set of beliefs that support government intervention in the economy to promote domestic interests and oppose the perceived drawbacks of globalization. In short, economic nationalism is a broad ideology emphasizing domestic economic interests over international ones. It has been revitalized in recent years due to the prevalence of skepticism regarding globalization, which economic nationalist policies aims to counteract.

Ostensibly, the ascent of an ideology based on national autonomy seems surprising in an otherwise increasingly international age with new technologies such as the internet connecting people all over the world. However, this growing network of global interactions and the challenges associated with it are in fact the very problem this movement seeks to solve. A backlash against a period of globalization, economic nationalism is an ideology aimed at mitigating the erosion of domestic control over economic affairs by means of protectionist and anti-globalist policies.

Economic nationalism is difficult to define because it does not fit neatly within any larger ideology, and different individuals and groups manifest it in disparate ways. Economist Dani Rodrik explained why he subscribes to this set of beliefs by writing simply that "democracies have the right to protect their social arrangements. And when this right clashes with the requirements of the global economy, it is the latter that should give way."[26] It is, after all, the duty of a state to defend its sovereignty, and by nature, a government's primary obligation remains to its own constituents rather than to the citizens of other states.

On the surface, economic nationalism seems rooted in this comprehensible philosophy, but when it comes to the implementation of specific economic nationalist policies, the ideology becomes more difficult to succinctly define. For example, President Donald Trump, a right-wing economic nationalist, insists that the United States should adopt a more aggressive policy toward other global powers, renegotiate trade deals, and increase public investment in infrastructure.

On the other hand, journalist Robert Kuttner, a left-wing economic nationalist who favors those same policies, claims that the president's appointment of several bankers to his cabinet and substitution of privatization for infrastructure

---

26 Robert Kuttner, "White Nationalism and Economic Nationalism," *The American Prospect*, October 10, 2017, accessed May 11, 2018, http://prospect.org/article/white-nationalism-and-economic-nationalism.

investment prevent his policies from fulfilling the true aims of their stated goals.[27]

Even the traditionally far-right National Rally party in France—formerly called the National Front—has recently taken to certain aspects of far-left economic thought in an effort to garner support from the working class. Bernard Monot, one of the architects of the party's economic policy asserted, "Inside France, we are liberal [but] beyond our borders, everything changes: we must fight the unfair competition imposed on us by global deregulation."[28]

With proponents and opponents ranging across the political spectrum and lacking a consistent vision for their ideology, the minutiae surrounding economic nationalism are highly nuanced. The lack of a unified economic nationalist agenda poses a considerable challenge to business leaders trying to figure out the ideology's implications for their enterprises. Throughout various views, however, runs a common theme: economic nationalism opposes the post-Cold War international order, perceives globalization as inimical to domestic prosperity, and values state intervention in the market to defend domestic interests.

---

27 Ibid.
28 Renaud Lambert, "Does the FN Have an Economic Strategy?" *Le Monde Diplomatique*, May 01, 2017, accessed May 11, 2018, https://mondediplo.com/2017/05/07FN.

It seems odd at first that such an ideology is experiencing a revitalization amid an era marked by pervasive global institutions and pluralism. Closer analysis reveals, however, that economic nationalism did not emerge despite globalism but rather because of it. In a sense, the revival of economic nationalism is a reaction against the contemporary global order brought into being by technological advances and neoliberalism.

To understand the rise of economic nationalism, one must first understand the rise of globalism. To this end, philosopher James Burnham created the term "managerial elite" to refer to the transnational group that amassed economic power during the twentieth century due to its control over the means of production.[29] Professor Michael Lind explained the role this group played in bringing globalism into being:

> Through the empowerment of multinational corporations and the creation of transnational supply chains, managerial elites disempowered national labor and national governments and transferred political power from national legislatures to executive agencies, transnational bureaucracies, and treaty organizations. ... Managerial minorities of Western nations

---

29 Michael Lind, "The New Class War," American Affairs Journal, August 06, 2017, accessed May 11, 2018, https://americanaffairsjournal.org/2017/05/new-class-war/.

have predictably run amok, using their near-mo-
nopoly of power and influence in all sectors ... to
enact policies that advantage their members to the
detriment of their fellow citizens.[30]

From the perspective of economic nationalists, then, the
managerial elite are both the agents and benefactors of globalization, amassing global power in the hands of the few at
the expense of the many. The emergence of this managerial
elite has produced a complex array of tangible consequences
worldwide, which economic nationalism seeks to alleviate.

One such consequence has been a decline in productivity
because, as Lind puts it, industries "have pursued profits
by methods other than technology-driven productivity
growth."[31] A specific example is labor arbitrage, or the unre-
stricted movement of different kinds of labor across borders
as a result of international market forces, resulting in the
massive immigration of workers from developing countries
to wealthy countries and the transfer of factories in the opposite direction. Labor arbitrage slows the rate of technological
progress as it increases firms' profits without incentivizing
them to innovate.[32]

---

30 Ibid.
31 Ibid.
32 Ibid.

Additionally, multinational corporations often take advantage of tax rates and subsidies that vary across borders by relocating to offshore tax havens such as Ireland and the Cayman Islands, also widening corporate profit margins without improving productivity.[33] Both labor arbitrage and tax-and-subsidy arbitrage lead to the managerial elite growing richer and more powerful at no apparent benefit to the rest of society, a frustrating result for many in the latter group.

An economic nationalist would likely respond by creating incentives such as subsidies for firms that choose to remain domestic and deterrents such as increased duties and regulations for ones that choose to relocate their operations abroad. Such policies may coerce firms to limit their foreign operations or avoid expanding internationally entirely. By extension, they make international corporate social responsibility more difficult. When a company no longer has stakeholders in a given country, its incentive to prioritize the interests of the people living there is at best significantly reduced and at worst completely eliminated.

Subscribers to the economic nationalist philosophy contend that globalization has negatively affected the job market. They believe the emergence of global supply chains has harmed domestic workers as these chains depend mainly on

---

33   Ibid.

hands-on manufacturing labor from developing countries and on white-collar, service-sector labor from developed countries.[34]

Economic nationalists like Trump also note that in the United States, jobs have disappeared *en masse* from the manufacturing sector because this type of labor is more affordable overseas. For this reason, many blue-collar workers in the United States have taken up the cause of economic nationalism to defend their job security.

Even the service-sector jobs that remain cannot employ the country's entire workforce, especially because it is "the most inessential part" of the global supply chain according to economic nationalist Christopher Caldwell. "After all, there are many equally good ways to design clothes, decorate office spaces, or structure corporate hierarchies. Other countries' elites are willing to pay for the *American* way of doing those things because it shows them to be tied to wealth, power, and chic. A lot of what Americans think of as valuable service-sector know-how is actually mere prestige."[35] In other words, even though the remaining jobs provide generous salaries, they are scarce and lack security. Economic nationalists

---

34 Christopher Caldwell, "Sending Jobs Overseas," The Claremont Institute, Winter 2017, accessed May 11, 2018, http://www.claremont.org/crb/article/sending-jobs-overseas/.

35 Ibid.

therefore posit that even workers in this sector have sufficient reason to resist globalization as well.

Thus, for millions of American workers in various professions, globalization's threat to job markets in developed countries represents a substantial reason to support economic nationalism, as well as to be hostile toward any businesses seemingly promoting the interests of the global community over those of the national community.

Economic nationalists would likely prescribe the implementation of higher taxes or similar punitive measures against firms engaged in outsourcing. However, their argument overlooks several crucial facts. First, although outsourcing has driven many jobs overseas, the extent of this phenomenon has been greatly overstated, and the U.S. role in global free trade has resulted in a tremendous net gain of jobs. In fact, in January 2019, the United States enjoyed its hundredth consecutive month of job growth, and the unemployment rate has never remained below four percent for so long since the 1960s.[36], [37] This job growth has been recorded across most

---

36 Natalie Kitroeff, "Unemployment Rate Hits 3.9%, a Rare Low, as Job Market Becomes More Competitive," *The New York Times*, May 04, 2018, accessed May 11, 2018, https://www.nytimes.com/2018/05/04/business/economy/jobs-report.html.

37 Dominic Rushe, "US Economy Adds Jobs for Record 100th Consecutive Month," The Guardian (Guardian News and Media, February 1, 2019), https://www.theguardian.com/business/2019/feb/01/us-jobs-report-news-latest-record-breaking-month-100th-in-a-row.

industries in the United States and been accompanied by wage growth as well.[38] On the surface, nationalist rhetoric against outsourcing is sound, but these statistics severely undermine the claim that globalization leads to widespread job loss.

Furthermore, although nationalists belittle the quality of service-sector jobs and claim that Americans play an inessential role in the global supply chain, Dr. Panos Mourdoukoutas, professor of economics at Long Island University, believes just the opposite. He explained that "globalization allowed America to maintain its lead in innovation ... Popular products like Nike sneakers and Apple's smartphones and iPads may be made in China or elsewhere in Asia, but they are designed here, generating highly paid jobs for American employees and hefty returns for American investors."[39] Despite nationalist claims to the contrary, U.S. workers occupy the most essential part of the global supply chain, creating the designs upon which foreign workers depend for their own jobs. Working in the most lucrative positions while others work for significantly lower wages, Americans

---

38 Matthew Tarpey, "3 Things to Know about the April 2019 Jobs Report," CareerBuilder, 2019, https://www.careerbuilder.com/advice/bls-jobs-report.

39 Panos Mourdoukoutas, "Globalization Has Done a Lot of Great Things for Americans," *Forbes*, January 04, 2017, accessed May 11, 2018, https://www.forbes.com/sites/panosmourdoukoutas/2017/01/03/globalization-has-done-many-great-things-for-americans/#57df2e93583d.

can also easily afford to consume these globally constructed products at prices so low that they would be unsustainable to produce domestically.

One example Dr. Mourdoukoutas pointed to is Apple. In 2014, the iPhone 5 sold for between $650 and $850, but Andrew Rassweiler, senior director of materials and cost benchmarking at IHS Markit, estimates that an identical iPhone entirely produced in the United States would cost the consumer around $2,000.[40] As we have already discussed, Apple outsources its manufacturing to Foxconn, a serial perpetrator of supply chain abuses in China. When done responsibly, however, outsourcing can help companies succeed without mistreating their stakeholders.

In 2016, for example, Levi's "original fit selvedge jeans" sold for around $128, while the same kind of jeans in the same fit from Levi's "Made in America" collection were listed online for $348, over two-and-a-half times the cost of the pair made abroad.[41] But the mere fact that Levi Strauss & Co.

---

40 Stacey Vanek Smith, "How Much Would an All-American IPhone Cost?" *Marketplace*, May 20, 2014. https://www.marketplace.org/2014/05/20/business/ive-always-wondered/how-much-would-all-american-iphone-cost.

41 Dana Varinsky, "Here's What 5 of Your Favorite Products Would Cost If They Were Made in the US," *Business Insider*. Business Insider, November 27, 2016. https://www.businessinsider.com/how-much-products-would-cost-if-made-in-us-2016-11#jeans-2.

outsources its manufacturing to save money on labor costs does not mean it is an irresponsible company.

In fact, it stands out in its industry as a leader in social responsibility. Levi Strauss enforces a self-imposed restricted substances list, which enumerates potentially hazardous chemicals the company banned from its products to protect consumers, employees, and the environment; it assists in the International Labor Organization's campaign to improve factory working conditions; it issues grants to women in its factories; and it educates apparel workers in more than forty countries about HIV/AIDS prevention.[42]

"If you really want to improve workers' lives," Erika Fry wrote in an article for *Fortune*, "why not just pay them more? Levi's [says] that their workers make more than the minimum [which in Mexico is about $5 per day for garment workers], plus fringe benefits, and that higher wages didn't top the list of priorities in employee surveys."[43] Outsourcing has enabled the company to uphold not only its responsibility to its customers by keeping prices much lower than they otherwise would be, but also its responsibility to its workers in other countries who work in decent conditions for

---

42 "Source," Levi Strauss & Co., https://www.levistrauss.com/suppliers-operations/.

43 Erika Fry, "Can Levi's Make Life Better for Garment Workers?" Fortune, September 8, 2017, http://fortune.com/2017/09/08/levis-change-the-world.

competitive wages. Where Apple fell short, Levi's succeeded and proved that global supply chains are not necessarily inimical to social responsibility as some economic nationalists claim.

GETTING POLITICAL

Regardless of corporate leaders' personal beliefs, politically motivated CSR remains ill-advised because it can render a government vulnerable to manipulation and corruption. For example, in 2011, a team of CSR experts in the United Kingdom found that British-American Tobacco (BAT) used its CSR programs as a lobby to rally enough political support to avoid harsh tobacco regulations, and "under the guise of political CSR, several [multinational corporations export] military hardware to oppressive governments [and] give bribes to politicians in developing nations."[44] The focus, then, should be on skill-building rather than democracy-building. Under political CSR, a corporation can compel a state to behave in a certain way, but this is less effective for developing a healthy democracy than skill-building, which provides stakeholders with the tools they need to contribute to their country's economic and political development.

---

44 "Political Corporate Social Responsibility and Development," Ismail Adelopo, Kemi Yekini, and Lukman Raimi, http://eprints. uwe.ac.uk/26635/1/Political%20Corporate%20Social%20Responsibility%20and%20Development.docx

It is commonly accepted that all nations have a right to self-determination.

Still, people throughout the world may see merit in economic nationalism due to globalization's alleged incompatibility with the natural volatility of democratic politics. After all, as Caldwell suggested, "the global economy is a fair-weather economy. If there is a slight rise in tariffs, a subtle judicial reinterpretation of regulation, a tiny change of attitude—in short, if there is any exercise of what we think of as normal democracy anywhere along the supply chain—the model … will fall apart."[45] He makes a fair point. The global economy involves countless moving parts, and the ever-changing nature of democracy adds an element of chaos to the scene. Because power changes hands so frequently, it is difficult to determine whether a democratic country will maintain its current economic commitments following each election. In such an intricate global system of trade, this reality can create a great deal of uncertainty.

While the allegation that the natural trappings of democracy will cause the underpinnings of a globalized economy to collapse may be a somewhat hyperbolic claim, you can easily envision a scenario in which a drastic change in one country's government may send supply chains spiraling into

---

45   Caldwell, "Sending Jobs Overseas."

disarray. Following the economic nationalist line of argument, then, a state should do everything in its power to maintain domestic control over all aspects of production through the use of protectionist policies such as import quotas.

However, not only would such policies result in market inefficiency and likely raise costs for multinational corporations and, by extension, domestic consumers, but the fear of "a slight rise in tariffs" causing an entire supply chain to "fall apart" is still largely misguided. Political forces, including ones from abroad such as wars, terror attacks, and regime changes, have long resulted in the temporary distortion of international markets, which always eventually recover.

If, hypothetically, a democratic state exports a resource for use in a global supply chain, and that state raises its export tariffs, the state importing that resource would recognize that its business was no longer tenable and begin importing it from another state. Having lost this source of income as a result of poor policymaking, the citizens of the first country would become worse off and logically vote out the party responsible for raising the tariff that pushed prices to a prohibitive level, and the supply chain would return to its original state within a few years.

Contrary to Caldwell's claim, the supply chain would not implode but adapt as all markets do. While inevitable market fluctuations undoubtedly pose a threat to the success of businesses of any size and may impair their ability to promote social good by limiting their resources, such fluctuations are only temporary; affected businesses either recover or are eventually replaced by more efficient ones. The dynamic, citizen-driven nature of democracies makes them fully compatible with a globalized market, from which the implementation of protectionist policies would only serve to isolate them.

The primary danger for multinational corporations, then, lies in undemocratic countries, where governments unaccountable to their people can enact disruptive economic policies without concern for public opinion. Therein arises another problem for corporate social responsibility: many of the world's poorest countries, in which many global supply chains base their resource extraction, manufacturing, and IT-enabled services, are ruled by oppressive, illiberal regimes.

Professor Michael Ryan of Georgetown University's McDonough School of Business laid out the challenges associated with operating in such a setting:

> Companies that provide money to set up schools or health clinics [find that these] are the kinds of projects that put them at the mercy of the institutional environment. It's easy to fail in this environment. That's the nature of a developing economy with

malfunctioning institutions. When you're making a contribution aimed at a local activity, it's difficult to succeed. Running your own business is something you know how to do, and you have control. You enter a particular country and have an idea of how things should be. If you're investing in building a school or a clinic, then a lot of factors are out of your control. In a lot of these settings, anything can go wrong.

Business leaders may feel concerned about operating in undemocratic countries and attempt to promote democratic institutions as part of their social responsibility undertaking, but it's best for companies to avoid political ends like this, and not only because they risk alienating stakeholders by stepping into politics.

Corporations are ill-suited for building governments. As Elzbieta Krzanowski put it, "Sometimes people mistake skill-building for democracy-building. … We need to let them learn for the benefit of their countries and our world. We all want to live in a better-educated, more peaceful, better-functioning world, and education is the most important part of that. But we can't pretend we know best. There are cultural, structural, and religious differences. We can't insist on anything. We can only present our knowledge and hope that those we address will learn from it and adapt to better themselves and to better the world." A company can be trusted to help with economic development of a country, but it can't be trusted with the liberalization of a country's government. "Democracy, brought to you by Coca-Cola®" is not truly democracy, because it requires a foreign, private entity to influence the public sphere, which is fundamentally undemocratic.

In other words, companies should not play a direct role in a host country's politics, as this would constitute a violation of that country's sovereign right to self-determination. A corporation can, however, steer a country toward the right track by promoting greater education and wealth there, arming its citizens with the proper tools to build the foundation of liberalization themselves.

As Andreas-Georg Scherer and Guido Palazzo explain in research published in *The Journal of Management Studies*, "The growing engagement of business firms in public policy leads to concerns of a democratic deficit… [N]ational governments are partly losing their regulatory influence over globally stretched corporations while some of those corporations, under the pressure of civil society, start to regulate themselves."[46] This decreases the relative regulatory power of

---

46 Scherer, Andreas-Georg, and Guido Palazzo. "The New Political Role of Business in a Globalized World: A Review of a New Perspective on CSR and Its Implications for the Firm, Governance, and Democracy." Journal of Management Studies. John Wiley &

democratically elected governments. Meanwhile, a self-regulating private enterprise headed by an unelected manager unaccountable to the citizens of a country operates without any form of democratic legitimacy or external checks and balances. Ultimately, politically motivated corporate social responsibility, even when well-intentioned, is detrimental to democracy and should therefore be avoided.

Corporations must carefully tread the line between modernizing societies and Westernizing them. They have a social responsibility to respect the sovereignty of their host nations while also contributing in one way or another to their development. While nationalists contend that globalization represents a detrimental force for international politics and economics, this is not necessarily the case. When approached correctly, international companies can use CSR to simultaneously advance their own interests and the interests of the countries they operate in, contributing to a united corporate and global good.

Sons, Ltd (10.1111), April 27, 2011. https://onlinelibrary.wiley.com/doi/full/10.1111/j.1467-6486.2010.00950.x.

PART II

THE WRONG
AND THE RIGHT

CHAPTER 3

LESSONS FROM POORLY EXECUTED CSR

Why is international CSR so important in the first place? After all, don't all companies contribute to society in every place they operate by paying taxes and creating jobs? Many proponents of laissez-faire capitalism continue to uphold economic philosopher Milton Friedman's notion of a corporation fulfilling its social obligations simply by turning a profit.

The fact of the matter is that CSR has become obligatory for international companies. Take, for example, India, which in 2013 enacted a law compelling companies to contribute at least 2 percent of their net profits to local social causes or publicly explain the reasons for their failure to do so.[47] Even companies not subject to such laws feel increasing pressure to engage in CSR activities in order to compete publicly with those that do. "For modern business, an ethical supply chain is no longer merely a 'feel good' PR tool," representatives of the international law firm K&L Gates explained. "Rather, it is rapidly becoming the standard required of companies by consumers, shareholders, lenders, litigants, and also more commonly, sovereigns. Multi-national corporations with global supply chains are facing increasing disclosure obligations and risk of misconduct by their suppliers, including involvement in human trafficking, forced labor, and human rights abuses. This kind of misconduct in a supply chain not only offends notions of human dignity and good corporate citizenship, but it can also result in severe damage to the company's brand(s), loss of goodwill, lost profits, shareholder value, diminished access to capital, and even fines and penalties."[48]

---

47 "Taking Stock of India's Mandatory CSR Legislation Four Years Out," Taking Stock of India's Mandartory CSR Legislation Four Years Out (The Kenan Institute for Ethics at Duke University, August 23, 2018), https://kenan.ethics.duke.edu/csr-workshop/.

48 Caitlin C. Blanche et al., "Global Supply Chain Risk: Corporate Exposure for Human Trafficking, Forced Labor and Human Rights Abuses | Stay Informed | K&L Gates," K&L Gates LLP, October 24, 2017, http://www.klgates.com/global-supply-chain-risk-corporate-exposure-for-human-trafficking-forced-labor-and-human-rights-abuses-10-24-2017/.

Yet, despite facing increasing pressure to maintain active social responsibility, many contemporary international organizations still struggle to do so even when they dedicate significant resources to that end. While they ostensibly contribute to global progress, many still fail to achieve substantive advancement for a number of reasons. One cause is the growing trend of companies who try to do too much for social responsibility. Firms that overreach often find themselves not only falling short of their established goals but ultimately harming the companies and the global stakeholders they seek to protect. Failing to account for institutional differences between their home country and the other countries in which they operate, these companies sometimes engage in programs to combat social issues that are simply beyond their ability to solve.

I asked Georgetown professor Michael Ryan how even well-meaning international companies can fail to spur real social change. "Companies that provide money to set up schools or health clinics are the kinds of projects that put them at the mercy of the institutional environment of the country they are operating in," he elucidated. It is rare that the local country can provide the structural support needed to sustain these programs, so they fail. "That's the nature of a developing economy with malfunctioning institutions. When you're making [a contribution] aimed at a local activity, those are difficult to make successful. Running your own business is something you know how to do, and you have control. You enter a particular country and have an idea of how things should be, but if you're investing in building a school or a clinic, then a lot of things are out of your control. In a lot of these settings, many factors can go wrong."

Many companies fail to realize this fact until it is too late and they have already launched a development program in a country that cannot offer the institutional provisions to help the project realize its intended purpose. Although an MNC might have the means to erect and staff a school, it almost certainly lacks the means to ensure that the initiative actually comes to fruition without the cooperation of the host country's government, which cannot be guaranteed without the powerful institutions primarily associated with already developed states.

In developing countries, a lack of transparency, together with governmental corruption, often thwarts the well-intentioned efforts of international companies. The CEO and managing partner of Proa Global Partners LLC, Harry G. Broadman, cited a 2011 incident "when two oil companies contributed an initial installment of $175 million (out of a promised total of $350 million) to establish a technical research and training center in Angola to be run by that country's state owned oil monopoly—Sonangol. Remarkably, more than six years later there is no such center and no one seems to know where the money actually went."[49]

Although these two companies likely sought to create social change and benefit financially from it, their project backfired, resulting in multiple investigations under the Foreign Corrupt Practices Act (FCPA).[50] The two companies behind this endeavor, BP and Cobalt, hail from the United Kingdom and United States, respectively. A BP representative told Quartz that corporate programs like this one are "like paying taxes—once you've paid your tax, you can't tell your government what to do with it."[51] As easy as it is, simply throwing money at developing countries will not solve their problems, and it will not make for effective CSR. In the case of Cobalt, this approach even resulted in an otherwise avoidable SEC investigation.[52]

49 Harry G. Broadman, "When Too Much Corporate Social Responsibility (CSR) Is Too Good To Be True," Forbes (Forbes Magazine, September 3, 2018), https://www.forbes.com/sites/harrybroadman/2018/05/30/when-too-much-corporate-social-responsibility-is-too-good-to-be-true/#290503be499f.

50 Ibid.

51 Tim Fernholz, "The Absence of a Mysterious Research Center in Angola Could Be Evidence of Oil Corruption," Quartz (Quartz, August 12, 2014), https://qz.com/247521/the-absence-of-a-mysterious-research-center-in-angola-could-be-evidence-of-oil-corruption/.

52 Ibid.

Corrupt public officials can take advantage of such international transactions, rerouting the flow of foreign financial resources away from the segment of the population in need of assistance to line the pockets of the elites instead. This only reinforces the unjust societal power structure that effective international CSR should seek to disrupt, exacerbating the very instability that these companies had initially attempted to mitigate and creating an even more difficult environment for businesses to operate in.

CSR DONE POORLY

What does it even mean "to fail" at international CSR? Well, as one might expect given the lack of a universally accepted definition of CSR, there are varying degrees and a significant gray area in terms of CSR success. Take, for example, Paul Polman, CEO of the consumer goods conglomerate Unilever, which some observers have criticized as overreaching in its overseas CSR initiatives and, as a result, falling short. Former shareholder activist and business executive Dr. Tom Borelli alleged that "Polman's focus on social matters distracted him from addressing core business challenges."[53] To be sure, Borelli makes an important point that every business

---

53 Wayne Winegarden, "Unilever And The Failure Of Corporate Social Responsibility," Econostats (Forbes Magazine, March 15, 2017), https://www.forbes.com/sites/econostats/2017/03/15/unilever-and-the-failure-of-corporate-social-responsibility/#670eaf-c498d2.

leader, regardless of their level of commitment to CSR, must acknowledge: a company that gets too wrapped up in promoting the welfare of its stakeholders forgets about its primary obligation to them—the bottom line.

Polman has stated that "as CEO of Unilever, my personal mission is to galvanize our company to be an effective force for good."[54] While this goal was admirable, under Polman's leadership, the company became so deeply engrossed in his personal vision of global CSR that it overlooked key areas of CSR within the company. While Polman was focused on global sustainability, hundreds of workers at a thermometer plant in India suffered from exposure to mercury, numerous African workers claimed that they resorted to bribery to prevent their supervisors from sexually harassing them, and the company failed to realize its projected sales figures.[55] A business that can't succeed financially can't succeed in improving the world.

The sheer magnitude of international social issues can pose yet another a challenge to an altruistic, ambitious business leader. We live in an imperfect world where suffering is pervasive, but ultimately, Unilever demonstrates that one company can't solve all the world's problems, and if it tries,

---

54 Ibid.
55 Ibid.

it's likely to encounter problems of its own. It is thus crucial to maintain a narrow CSR focus and ensure that the bottom line is met, because profit acts as the foundation for everything the company seeks to achieve. An unprofitable company can't afford to look out for its stakeholders in the most basic of senses. Across the world, employees need wages, governments depend on tax revenue to operate, consumers demand products, and investors want a high return so they can reinvest it and help grow more enterprises. If the company does not generate a profit, these most basic needs go unmet. Milton Friedman wasn't entirely wrong when he famously declared in the *New York Times* in 1970, "The social responsibility of a business is to increase its profit." Borelli echoed many other critics who have all raised a valid point.

Humanity has neither a unified set of morals nor a consistent commitment to those morals, especially from one culture to the next, so it would be unreasonable to expect any organization of an international scale to possibly "do the right thing" 100 percent of the time. This makes it difficult to offer a universally applicable standard for international CSR. However, while it would be naive to expect perfection from massive companies made up of thousands of inherently flawed human beings, we can reasonably expect them to do their best.

Just as we cannot expect perfection from individuals, we cannot expect perfection from global networks of individuals. We can, however, demand their genuine strongest effort to be decent global citizens. This is, of course, a very subjective bar to meet. But given that infrequent moral mishaps are inevitable, we can still look to companies to prevent them from becoming a regularity and to effectively respond to them when they do occur. It is when corporate irresponsibility becomes less of an isolated incident and more of a recurring theme that concern should be raised regarding the systemic integrity of the organization.

CSR DONE WELL

As is always the case with the market, problems create a demand for maximally effective solutions. Broadman suggested "mainstreaming CSR and ESG [environmental, social, and governance] investment decision-making into the core of corporate growth strategy rather than hiving it off as an ancillary function, stove-piped into a business foundation, or worst, treated as an afterthought."[56] In other words, there are steps a company can take to avoid the fate of the oil companies in Angola. Internally, a company should implement a system of checks and balances to ensure thorough review of all social activities abroad. Externally, third parties can

---

56 Broadman, "Too Much CSR."

be hired to undertake legitimate audits of international CSR initiatives to evaluate their susceptibility to malfeasance and related forces. By executing both of these steps in conjunction with any overseas social program, corporations can significantly reduce the risk of CSR failure in areas with weak institutions.

Indeed, as Broadman says, for social responsibility to be successful, it cannot be some secondary consideration written into the postscript of a business's mission statement—it must be hardwired into the business itself. This is especially true on an international scale, where companies receive increased visibility. Some still disregard this wisdom and treat CSR as a function discrete from the daily operations and mission of the company.

In particularly glaring cases, a company may put on a façade of social responsibility directly inimical to the primary objective of the organization. A prominent example of this pseudo-CSR is when tobacco companies launch antismoking campaigns targeted at the youth of a population. Even though these campaigns ostensibly attempt to deter adolescents from smoking, they have the latent effect of portraying smoking as a forbidden fruit, so to speak. They depict tobacco use as an exclusively adult pleasure, increasing its allure in the eyes of young people. A report by the World Health Organization (WHO) explained,

Proposed measures that involve proof of age for purchase at the counter are ultimately ineffective, as young people easily circumvent these restrictions. Tactically, these [programs] serve the purpose of creating the appearance that tobacco companies are proposing solutions for the problems they create. In reality, they detract attention from proven, effective solutions—including price and tax increases—to which young people are particularly sensitive. Tobacco companies vigorously oppose price and tax increases.[57]

Like fast-food companies' anti-obesity campaigns, these programs are not truly socially responsible because they defy the very DNA of the companies behind them.

Implementing socially responsible programs to cover up or apologize for current or past misdeeds is in fact an example of irresponsibility. For example, McDonald's funding a social program to combat obesity is paradoxical in that it directly contradicts the daily operations of the company.[58] This is

---

57 "Tobacco Industry and Corporate Responsibility: an Inherent Contradiction," Tobacco Free Initiative (World Health Organization, 2004), http://www.who.int/tobacco/communications/CSR_report.pdf.

58 Samantha Gillison, "'Clean Eating' Is Such a Sham That Fast Food Chains Push It," NBC Opinion (NBCUniversal News Group, February 6, 2018), https://www.nbcnews.com/think/opinion/clean-eating-has-become-such-sham-fast-food-chains-are-ncna845081.

like BP pretending to be an environmental steward when in reality it is responsible for spilling millions of gallons of oil into the ocean—not true responsibility but rather a sham.[59] The good news for the world, though, is that stakeholders can often see through it.

CSR should not be a means to a bottom line; it should be an intrinsic part of the bottom line. Any CSR activity separate from a company's primary objective will lose out when it inevitably comes time for that company to make difficult decisions. Research from the *Harvard Business Review* shows that many companies practicing CSR enjoy lower wage demands from employees, as well as higher levels of employee retention and productivity.[60] This effect alone is enough to drive many firms to institute socially responsible business practices, but the same research yielded an even more fascinating conclusion. The researchers, Professors Stephan Meier and Lea Cassar, "found that if employees think their company is using CSR initiatives instrumentally — trying to engage in prosocial activities only to benefit from it — then they'll react negatively and put in less effort. In other

59 Andrew Price, "Why Companies Make False Corporate Social Responsibility Promises," Fast Company (Fast Company, February 21, 2012), https://www.fastcompany.com/1679334/why-companies-make-false-corporate-social-responsibility-promises.

60 Stephan Meier and Lea Cassar, "Stop Talking About How CSR Helps Your Bottom Line," Harvard Business Review (Harvard University, January 31, 2018), https://hbr.org/2018/01/stop-talking-about-how-csr-helps-your-bottom-line.

words, while these initiatives will benefit society, they will backfire for companies if people think they're being used for the wrong reasons."[61] In other words, stakeholders assess companies' actual intentions with significant accuracy and formulate highly consequential behaviors based on their perceived level of commitment to CSR.

This leaves two important takeaways for businesses: (1) by tying genuinely altruistic pursuits directly to the central mission of the company, they are more likely to reap advantages such as more highly motivated employees; and (2) they benefit from investing in effectively communicating their mission to stakeholders. The most successful instances of CSR are ones that align with the mission of the company. This is especially true for international corporations, which must strive to appease stakeholders the world over or risk failure.

---

61   Ibid.

CHAPTER 4

GOVERNMENTS AND INTERNATIONAL CSR

REGULATION

Many see international CSR as unimportant because governments are better equipped to solve problems of such a large
scale. Any action necessary on the corporation's part, they
argue, can simply be mandated by the government of the
country where the company is operating. On the surface, this
viewpoint makes sense, especially given the selfish nature
of private enterprises. Closer examination, however, reveals
that international CSR is in fact wholly necessary to build
a better future. International corporations and governments
should not be viewed as opposing forces in this regard and

should instead work in conjunction with one another to solve problems.

Some issues seem inherent in the global marketplace. For example, critics of globalization contend that competition between developing countries to attract foreign direct investment (FDI) from MNCs to stimulate economic growth creates a race to the bottom in terms of commercial regulations. One way this has occurred is through the advent of free trade zones (FTZs), areas where a government permits companies to manufacture, store, or export goods under reduced regulations and duties.[62] The lesser the regulations a country imposes on MNCs, the more they are incentivized to expand their operations there. Competition between countries to attract FDI, then, pressures them to lower their regulatory standards as much as possible. This presents a conundrum for socially responsible international companies, which would profit more by taking advantage of these decreased regulations but would in doing so betray their CSR commitments. In other words, a dilemma arises due to the conflicting interests of different stakeholders. On one hand, business owners and investors benefit from decreased regulations because of the resulting increase in profits. On the other hand, though, this may mean that customers or the

---

62 The Editors of Encyclopaedia Britannica, "Free-Trade Zone," Encyclopædia Britannica (Encyclopædia Britannica, inc., February 26, 2016), https://www.britannica.com/topic/free-trade-zone.

environment suffer because of decreased production standards, the host country misses out on lost tax revenue that could have been used to promote development, or employees work for longer hours in worse conditions.

While this dilemma may at first seem impossible to reconcile, closer analysis of the issue reveals that an international company does not need to sacrifice its social commitments to maximize its profits or vice versa. In fact, governmental regulation of MNCs is not the most efficient way to safeguard stakeholder interests. Rather, all parties are better off when companies hold themselves to high standards of social responsibility independent of those set by the state. While the idea of a private enterprise regulating itself may at first seem laughable, it is actually within an international company's best financial interest to establish and maintain a strong commitment to the welfare of the community supporting it.

For example, the government of a developing country desperate for FDI may choose to overlook a foreign company's environmental abuses. It is first worth noting that such abuses cause the most detriment in developing regions such as South Asia, where air pollution results in annual labor income losses costing nearly 1 percent of GDP.[63] According to Laura Tuck, vice president for sustainable development at

63 "Air Pollution Deaths Cost Global Economy US$225 Billion," World Bank (World Bank Group, September 8, 2016),

the World Bank, "Air pollution is a challenge that threatens basic human welfare, damages natural and physical capital, and constrains economic growth. ... By supporting healthier cities and investments in cleaner sources of energy, we can reduce dangerous emissions, slow climate change, and most importantly save lives."[64] The health of the environment is crucial to the economies of developing countries. This should alarm any company that maintains a stake in these economies.

Global warming has led to a recent upsurge in natural disasters. At the end of the last decade, a report from the United Nations Refugee Agency found that the total number of natural disasters on Earth had doubled in just twenty years.[65] These disasters cause not only the loss of human capital by claiming lives, but also the destruction of tangible assets such as buildings and equipment as well. The result is a tremendous loss in productivity. The UN Food and Agriculture Organization published a study calculating the global economic impact of natural disasters to total $1.5 trillion between 2003 and 2013, and the situation has only grown

---

http://www.worldbank.org/en/news/press-release/2016/09/08/air-pollution-deaths-cost-global-economy-225-billion.

64 Ibid.

65 "UNHCR Policy Paper: Climate Change, Natural Disasters and Human Displacement: a UNHCR Perspective," UNHCR (United Nations), accessed February 10, 2018, https://www.unhcr.org/4901e81a4.html.

worse since then.[66] The insurance firm Swiss Re estimates that 2017 was the costliest year ever, with natural disasters causing the global economy to lose over $300 billion in that year alone.[67] While international businesses may benefit in the short term from disregarding their ecological impact, they have a long-term vested interest in the health of the environment just like everyone else.

Critics of international CSR may maintain that it is the responsibility of governments, charitable organizations, and international institutions like the UN, rather than for-profit enterprises, to find solutions to worldwide challenges like climate change. On the contrary, though, their vast financial resources, constant pressure to optimize efficiency, and capacity for innovation make international companies well-suited to tackling these issues. The Swedish retail giant Ikea has already invested $2 billion in renewable energy and installed 750,000 solar panels on its buildings and in the future plans to build 426 wind turbines, terminate all of its single-use plastic products, and make its home delivery

---

66 "The Impact of Disasters on Agriculture and Food Security," Food and Agriculture Organization (United Nations, 2015), http://www. fao.org/3/a-i5128e.pdf.

67 "Natural Catastrophes and Climate Change," Swiss Re 2017 Corporate Responsibility Report (Swiss Re, 2017), http://reports.swissre. com/corporate-responsibility-report/2017/cr-report/solutions/natural-catastrophes-and-climate-change.html.

process 100 percent emissions-free.[68] Professors Michael Vandenbergh and Jonathan Gilligan highlighted another example in the U.S. Southeast, where most states "have litigated vigorously to prevent the federal government from enforcing national regulations that would reduce emissions from coal-fired power plants. Although these states are not pursuing carbon emissions reductions, Google, Facebook, and other companies are pushing utilities in the region to provide renewable energy for new facilities such as data centers and are extending their influence by encouraging other electricity buyers to do the same."[69] These international companies, acting in their own best interest and in the interest of their stakeholders, have greatly exceeded the environmental standards set for them by their host governments and affirmed that private enterprises have more to gain from embracing their social responsibility than they do from trying to sidestep it. As with all other international CSR commitments, the key is to treat environmental stewardship not as an encumbrance to the business, or even as an ancillary effort, but rather as an integral function.

---

68   Ivana Kottasová, "These Companies Are Leading the Fight against Climate Change," CNN (Cable News Network, October 9, 2018), https://www.cnn.com/2018/10/09/business/climate-change-companies/index.html.

69   Michael Vandenbergh, "Why Private 'Actors' Are Taking Center Stage on Climate Change," GreenBiz (GreenBiz Group Inc., December 9, 2017), https://www.greenbiz.com/article/why-private-actors-are-taking-center-stage-climate-change.

The same is true of international companies' responsibility to their workers and suppliers in the absence of government regulation. They can certainly try to cut costs by taking advantage of FTZs in developing countries or find other ways to shirk their commitment to their employees, and many MNCs do this. By capitalizing in the short-term on irresponsible practices, though, they undermine the morale, loyalty, and energy of many people supporting the business, which can have catastrophic effects—recall the mass suicide at Apple's Chinese manufacturer FoxConn. Companies can generate both financial and social progress by investing heavily in their workforce. Starbucks, for example, sources much of its coffee from Central America and Africa. Through its Global Farmer Fund, the company has invested tens of millions of dollars to finance sustainable incomes for hundreds of its providers in developing countries like Rwanda and Nicaragua, enabling some farmers to double their production and, by extension, their income.[70] Starbucks, in turn, gains a larger supply of coffee, more devoted providers who have the capital to grow their businesses, and a better public image.

---

70 "Investing in Coffee Communities," Starbucks Coffee Company (Starbucks Coffee Company), accessed December 28, 2018, https://www.starbucks.com/responsibility/community/farmer-support/social-development-investments.

Companies that tend to the interests of workers abroad can, by extension, inspire and motivate their domestic employees. Meghan Dwyer, a retail development manager for St. Frank, a San Francisco-based company that sells ethically sourced textiles hand-crafted by artisans across the planet, told Forbes that she admires her employer's "commitment to creating quality jobs for artisans working in under-resourced settings all around the world. I believe that it's through job creation that we'll be able to end the cycle of poverty, and I was inspired to work for a company that had social impact built into its core DNA."[71] These brands engage in socially responsible corporate practices not because of government mandates but simply because it's good business, and these practices have successfully helped local entrepreneurs spur economic development.

We can conclude, then, that while some MNCs continue to exploit weak government regulations abroad for short-term financial gains, an international business rationally considering its long-term interests should invest in CSR to optimize both its financial and societal outcomes. The underlying implication here is that government intervention in the CSR sphere is not as crucial as some make it out to be.

---

71 Marissa Peretz, "These Companies Prove You Can Be Socially Conscious And Profitable," Forbes (Forbes Magazine, December 19, 2017), https://www.forbes.com/sites/marissaperetz/2017/12/19/these-companies-prove-you-can-be-socially-conscious-and-profitable/#109c648a3b10.

Yet, as CSR has penetrated more and more states around the world, many governments have done more to mandate and regulate commercial benevolence. Once voluntary undertakings by morally upstanding businesses have increasingly become obligatory, but this trend has not rendered the benefits that its advocates might have expected it to. In a phenomenon that professors Gerlinde Berger-Walliser and Inara Scott refer to as the "legalization" or "hardening" of CSR, well-meaning governments have unintentionally undermined the very practices they sought to promote by effectively rendering the term "CSR" meaningless.[72] "As CSR hardens and becomes more legalized," the researchers concluded, "the lack of definition and contradictions inherent in the term 'CSR' create confusion, undermine genuine corporate efforts and commitments, and make it difficult, if not impossible, for researchers to study the phenomenon. If a term can signal either a moral duty or *no* moral duty, voluntary *or* involuntary actions, charity or *not* charity, it is of little use in providing guidance to corporate actors and boundaries to facilitate future study."[73] Each government or other regulatory body that tries to make CSR obligatory must define for itself what exactly constitutes CSR, which raises

---

72 Gerlinde Berger⊠Walliser and Inara Scott, "Redefining Corporate Social Responsibility in an Era of Globalization and Regulatory Hardening," American Business Law Journal (John Wiley & Sons, Ltd (10.1111), February 2, 2018), https://onlinelibrary.wiley.com/doi/full/10.1111/ablj.12119.

73 Ibid.

a number of philosophical questions on where the ethical responsibilities of a business begin and end. With every new attempt to legalize CSR arises a new definition of it, resulting in endless confusion. Ultimately, it is best left up to each individual business to decide for itself what its moral pursuits will be without the influence of governments.

The more CSR becomes a *legal obligation* of the corporation, the less it is a *social responsibility,* undercutting the traditional motivation for companies to behave ethically. CSR is most effective when closely linked with the core mission of a company. No company's mission is to simply obey the law. Market innovation should be tied to social innovation. If CSR becomes simply a portion of profits that must be donated to charity or compliance with carbon emissions levels set by the government, the innovative potential of companies is limited. The point is to bring about social change, not abide by the preexisting status quo. If all companies follow the same strictly enforced steps, governments will become the sole arbiter of social change—or stagnancy—in the world, defeating the purpose of CSR in the first place. CSR is not a government-issued checklist, but a search for solutions to global problems that demand inventive, competitive effort from millions of individual actors.

CORRUPTION

Perhaps another, more compelling reason for governments not to play a role in defining or regulating CSR is that the interests of public officials often conflict with or even taint the social objectives of international companies. In other words, sometimes, especially in the case of developing countries, the governments themselves are the problem. The ongoing worldwide bribery scandal of the German conglomerate Siemens AG represents a prime example of government embroilment in international corporate irresponsibility. Investigations beginning in 2005 uncovered that representatives of the company had administered tens of millions of dollars in bribes every year to curry favor with public officials all over the world and win highly sought-after government contracts in Greece, Bangladesh, Vietnam, Mexico, Iraq, Nigeria, Israel, Russia, China, Argentina, and Venezuela.[74] In all, Siemens was forced to pay $1.6 billion in fines to Germany and the United States, as well as an additional $1 billion for internal investigations and restructuring, and this doesn't even account for the potential future business opportunities the company has consequently lost.[75] When Siemens tried to profit from corruption, it ended up significantly worse-off as a result.

---

74 Siri Schubert and T. Christian Miller, "At Siemens, Bribery Was Just a Line Item," The New York Times (The New York Times, December 20, 2008), https://www.nytimes.com/2008/12/21/business/worldbusiness/21siemens.html.

75 Ibid.

This is not just a matter of corporate responsibility, but one of social responsibility as well. Guillermo C. Jimenez and Elizabeth Pulos wrote in their book *Good Corporation, Bad Corporation*, "In January 2010 Alcatel agreed to pay Costa Rica US $10 million in reparations for social damage caused by Alcatel's payment of US$2.5 million in bribes to get a contract to provide mobile phone services in that country. This case is notable for its application of the concept of *social damage* and the resulting order of compensation to the citizens of Costa Rica."[76] This precedent makes clear that any act of corruption is a violation of both the law *and* any company's social obligations.

But combating corruption as a function of CSR can create shared value for both the corporation and the host country. Widespread corruption deters investors from supporting undertakings in developing countries; it also results in the skimming of corporate revenue to line the pockets of unscrupulous officials and the diversion of public resources away from development programs. Moreover, it can unfairly skew competition in a manner detrimental to the free market while increasing the costs and risks of doing business. Because corruption inhibits the proper functioning of corporations and governments alike, their mutual best interest lies in uprooting it.

---

76 Jimenez, *Good Corporation, Bad Corporation.*

A report by the social impact consulting firm FSG explained, "Corruption not only poses real costs to businesses (including operational costs, legal risks, and competitive risks) but also exacts significant costs on society (including reduced government services for the disadvantaged, constraints on foreign direct investment in high-corruption countries, and crime and instability resulting from decreased trust in government)."[77]

While the leadership at Siemens failed to operate under this logic, the German pharmaceutical company Merck & Co. has made a point to integrate it into its CSR activities. Amid an industry with an otherwise poor CSR record, Merck has made great strides against corruption, having invested millions of dollars to establish nonprofit ethics centers in four different countries.[78] The company elaborated in its anti-corruption report that "Merck's rationale was to create a true overlap of business and societal interests: as business transactions became more transparent and less corrupt, Merck would benefit because it could compete based on the quality of its products alone."[79] Both the company and the countries in which it operates can benefit from reduced corruption.

---

77 Greg Hills, Leigh Fiske, and Adeeb Z. Mahmud, "Anti-Corruption as Strategic CSR: A Call to Action for Corporations," FSG (FSG Social Impact Advisors, July 17, 2018), https://www.fsg.org/publications/anti-corruption-strategic-csr#download-area.

78 Ibid.

79 Ibid.

Although governments of developing countries often struggle to rid themselves of corruption, this case demonstrates that assistance can come from international actors in the private sector for the good of the actor itself and of society as a whole.

But Merck is not alone in its commitment to stop corruption. In fact, the International Chamber of Commerce (ICC)—the most diverse business organization in the world, with six million members in over 130 countries—has published numerous publicly available guidelines on whistleblowing, conflicts of interest, and resisting extortion and solicitation in international transactions.[80] The ICC, too, has a vested interest in fighting global corruption, which, in its own words, "threatens the integrity of markets, undermines fair competition, distorts resource allocation, destroys public trust and undermines the rule of law," all dangers that are bad for both business and society.[81] Yet the issue is not as simple as it first appears.

Bribery, for example, represents a quintessential form of corruption that is especially relevant to global businesses. According to the OECD Convention on Combating Bribery of Foreign Public Officials in International Business

---

80 "Combatting Corruption," ICC (International Chamber of Commerce), accessed December 23, 2018, https://iccwbo.org/global-issues-trends/responsible-business/combatting-corruption/.
81 Ibid.

Transactions, while international companies may commit bribery abroad, they typically conduct the bulk of their accounting in their home countries.[82] Bribery thus puts multinationals at the mercy of multiple different states at once. But even if we suppose that a company may be able to circumvent legal repercussions for bribery, it still has several compelling reasons to avoid it.

Primarily, corruption begets a dangerous environment for businesses. In Mexico, for example, Ernst & Young's 2018 Global Fraud Survey found that corruption affects the daily operations of more than two-thirds of companies. According to the GAN Business Anti-Corruption Portal, "Business registration processes, including getting construction permits and licenses, are negatively influenced by corruption. Organized crime continues to be a very problematic factor for business, imposing large costs on companies. Collusion between the police, judges and criminal groups is extensive, leading to widespread crime, theft, impunity and weak law enforcement."[83]

---

82 "CONVENTION ON COMBATING BRIBERY OF FOREIGN PUBLIC OFFICIALS IN INTERNATIONAL BUSINESS TRANSACTIONS," OECD (The Organisation for Economic Co-operation and Development, 2011), http://www.oecd.org/daf/anti-bribery/ ConvCombatBribery_ENG.pdf, 17.

83 "Mexico Corruption Report," Business Anti-Corruption Portal (GAN Integrity, Inc., 2018), https://www.business-anti-corruption. com/country-profiles/mexico/.

The irregular application of the law by an inefficient judiciary and police force allows for the violation of property rights, inconsistent taxation, unreliable access to public services, and the expansion of violence. Altogether, these factors impose a heavy burden on businesses operating in the country. According to the World Economic Forum's 2017 Executive Opinion Survey, in fact, corruption is the single greatest obstacle to doing business in Mexico, more problematic than tax regulations, access to financing, and inadequate infrastructure combined.[84]

This is particularly relevant for international companies, which must deal significantly with the corruption of Mexico's customs agency. Per a 2016 government estimate, "corrupt activities" occurred in 1,157 out of every 10,000 import and export transactions, yet the customs administration referred only thirty-four of its employees to the public prosecutor from 2016 through the first half of 2017.[85] This problem is widespread, negatively affecting both Mexican society and the international companies operating there, and the government is failing to resolve it. This leaves corporations with a choice: they can try to fight corruption themselves, or they can "play along" with it and try to use it to their advantage.

---

84 Klaus Schwab and Xavier Sala-i-Martín, "The Global Competitiveness Report 2017-2018," Insight Report (World Economic Forum, 2017), http://www3.weforum.org/docs/GCR2017-2018/05FullReport/ TheGlobalCompetitivenessReport2017–2018.pdf.

85 "Mexico Corruption Report."

Retail giant Walmart chose the latter option. Internal and external investigations uncovered evidence of bribes totaling $24 million, allegedly to facilitate the process of obtaining permits to open new stores throughout Mexico.[86] As of August 2018, the company had spent roughly $900 million on the ongoing legal battle and a global compliance overhaul; it set aside an additional $300 million in anticipation of a possible resolution.[87] In addition, when the scandal was first publicized, the company's stock value plummeted by $4.5 billion.[88] This long, costly affair draining Walmart's legal, public relations, and financial resources could have been avoided easily had the company simply opted not to pay these bribes.

To be fair, though, corruption is the norm in Mexico. Walmart made the easy decision not to challenge the status quo. However, in business as in life, the easy decision is not always the right one. Partaking in corruption perpetuates a culture that exacts costs both social and literal. Paying bribes only feeds into this culture, to the detriment of business and society. According to a 2015 report by Control Risks, "an overwhelming majority of companies in Mexico

---

86 Jimenez, *Good Corporation, Bad Corporation.*
87 Tom Schoenberg, "Walmart Deadlocked With U.S. Over Bribery Probe," Bloomberg.com (Bloomberg, August 2, 2018), https://www.bloomberg.com/news/articles/2018-08-02/walmart-is-said-to-be-deadlocked-with-u-s-over-bribery-probe.
88 Jimenez, *Good Corporation, Bad Corporation.*

believe that resisting demands of bribery by corrupt officials has a positive effect, as officials eventually become less likely to issue demands in the future."[89] By giving in and paying bribes, companies only reinforce a corrupt system that harms them and their host countries.

Fortunately, an alternative option exists. Ravi Venkatesan and Leslie Benton wrote in the *Harvard Business Review* that companies actively working against corruption benefit from a competitive advantage: "Fighting bribery builds reputation and brand value. Companies that can demonstrate conformity to an internationally-accepted anti-bribery standard may more easily attract business partners and investors who expect greater financial transparency and disclosure of activities to determine bribery risks."[90] MNCs can voluntarily undergo audits by third parties and request audits of their partners as well to ensure compliance with international standards such as those outlined by the ISO 37001.

During a 2010 internal review of its global anti-corruption practices, the Ralph Lauren Corporation found evidence that one of its subsidiaries in Argentina had bribed public officials there. The company promptly and completely

89 "Mexico Corruption Report."
90 Ravi Venkatesan and Leslie Benton, "How Companies Can Take a Stand Against Bribery," Harvard Business Review (Harvard University, September 17, 2018), https://hbr.org/2018/09/how-companies-can-take-a-stand-against-bribery.

divulged this evidence to the U.S. Department of Justice and the Securities and Exchange Commission. As a result of Ralph Lauren's responsible reporting and cooperation, the government ordered the company to pay fines totaling less than $2 million, a paltry sum compared to Walmart's expensive scandal.[91] Because Ralph Lauren reacted responsibly, it easily salvaged its brand and hardly lost anything in fines.

Battling corruption is no easy task, however: even some of the world's most powerful governments have fallen short. In China, for example, the drug manufacturer GlaxoSmith-Kline (GSK) came under fire for bribery in 2013. GSK first claimed that rogue individuals within the company had initiated the bribes, but it was later revealed that GSK itself had in fact orchestrated and paid the bribes. According to Guillermo Jimenez and Elizabeth Pulos, authors of the book *Good Corporation, Bad Corporation*, Chinese authorities further stated that "the corporate parent merely went through the motions of an internal audit process, indicating a knowledge and acceptance of the bribery. This very recent case suggests that the Chinese government's widely publicized arrests and convictions for bribery have not yet served as a sufficient deterrent to corrupt practices by foreign corporations."[92] Multinational corporations must do their part

---

91   Ibid.
92   Jimenez, *Good Corporation, Bad Corporation.*

to fight corruption because government regulations have proven insufficient.

This responsibility does not just encompass regular audits and internal investigations. Companies can battle corruption through more traditional CSR endeavors as well. A 2013 study by the Center for Economic Policy Research concluded, "Both theoretical and empirical evidence show that economic growth causes the amount of corruption to fall."[93] The higher a country's real GDP per capita, the lower its degree of corruption. Therefore, cpmote economic growth in their host countries. This improves a company's public image rather than tarnishing it and helps to weaken the obstacles imposed by corruption throughout the entire country, not just within the corporation itself. If companies invest in development instead of bribery, they better serve their own long-term interests. Where governments fail to generate social good, international corporations can succeed for the good of themselves and their stakeholders.

---

93 Jie Bai, Edmund Malesky, and Benjamin Olken, "Growing out of Corruption," Center for Economic Policy Research: Policy Portal (VOX, November 22, 2013), https://voxeu.org/article/growing-out-corruption.

CHAPTER 5

PATAGONIA

———

Disclaimer: This chapter relies heavily on information related to the clothing company Patagonia—strictly because of the company's CSR record. As of this writing, I have never received any form of compensation from Patagonia or any other brand named in this book except for Georgetown University, where I was once employed as a student worker. Moreover, I have never made agreements with any brands in exchange for favorable portrayal in this book.

With so many companies falling short of creating real progress in the world, it's easy to lose faith in business as a driver of global social change. While people on one side of the spectrum make assertions about the supposed malevolence of capitalism and those on the other side condemn globalism as a source of evil, you're left wondering whether international corporate social responsibility is worth discussing. Thankfully, a handful of business leaders have shone through as titans of both industry and altruism, proving that international corporate social responsibility is still a realistic ideal worth fighting for.

Perhaps the most prominent among these success stories is U.S.-based clothing company Patagonia, widely regarded as a global leader in CSR. Patagonia has defied the negative reputation of the global clothing industry, which is infamous for its widespread environmental and labor abuses, and instead proven that as long as the core function of the company itself is not inherently socially irresponsible,[i] there is nothing preventing that company from doing well by doing good. Patagonia's vast CSR undertakings include becoming the first brand to join bluesign system partners, having most of its annual material volume approved by a third party to ensure the chemicals, finishes, and dyes are safe for the environment, employees, and consumers;[94] undergoing an audit to receive accreditation from the Fair Labor Association to protect the rights of workers worldwide; maintaining generous benefits including health insurance for all full- and part-time employees; donating 100 percent of Black Friday sales ($10 million) to environmental organizations; and repairing

---

94 "Our DWR Problem [Updated]," The Cleanest Line (Patagonia, September 8, 2015), http://www.patagonia.com/blog/2015/09/our-dwr-problem-updated/.

tens of thousands of garments at dozens of repair facilities worldwide to prevent unnecessary waste.[95] Clearly, global businesses have something to learn from Patagonia's example.

To this end, I interviewed Vincent Stanley, co-author of *The Responsible Company* and the director of philosophy at Patagonia. Vincent first started working for Patagonia when the company was founded in 1973 and in that time has served as its head of sales and marketing, so he knows Patagonia's social responsibility efforts better than just about anyone.

Vincent explained that while the company has long been a leader in international CSR, it still seeks to constantly improve as much as possible. In fact, it recently went so far as to change its mission statement to emphasize its renewed commitment to social responsibility. The old mission statement, "Build the best product, cause no unnecessary harm, use business to inspire and implement solutions to the environmental crisis," was furloughed in favor of the simpler yet more powerful "We're in business to save our home planet."

For many, the original business statement sounds responsible enough. After all, building the best product is something

---

95 "Fiscal Year 2017," Annual Benefit Corporation Report 2017 (Patagonia, 2018), https://www.patagonia.com/static/on/demandware. static/-/Library-Sites-PatagoniaShared/default/dw824facof/PDF-US/2017-BCORP-pages_022218.pdf.

every business should aspire to; avoiding unnecessary harm should be a given, as anyone with an inkling of compassion lives their daily life without harming others unnecessarily; and creating solutions to the environmental crisis is absolutely necessary for the long-term preservation of life on Earth. These standards were simply not enough for the company. As Patagonia's founder, Yvon Chouinard, wrote in his book *Let My People Go Surfing*, "Evil doesn't have to be an overt act; it can be merely the absence of good. If you have the ability, the resources, and the opportunity to do good and you do nothing, that can be evil."[96] International companies like Patagonia have tremendous power to do good, and if they do not wield that power accordingly, their inaction constitutes injustice.

Thus Patagonia's original mission statement did not quite express the same commitment to CSR we see in the company today. Simply providing the best product does not necessarily mean that a company is doing everything it can to look out for its community, its employees, or even its customers. The avoidance of unnecessary harm suggests that some harm may be deemed necessary, but who arbitrates that? And while inspiring and implementing solutions to the environmental

---

96 Yvon Chouinard and Brendan Leonard, "17 Great Yvon Chouinard Quotes," Essays (Adventure Journal, November 11, 2014), https://www.adventure-journal.com/2014/11/the-aj-list-17-great-yvon-chouinard-quotes/.

crisis is certainly a noble cause, there are an array of other issues plaguing the company's stakeholders in the short term. Clearly, as the company grew, so too did the need for innovation in its CSR commitments.

"We're in business to save our home planet." The genius of this new, straightforward statement sets an example for other business leaders seeking to make a difference on a global scale. It acknowledges right away that Patagonia is, first and foremost, a business. And it has succeeded in this regard— as *The Guardian* reported, Patagonia "had sales of $800m in 2016, twice as much as in 2010, and has 29 standalone stores in the US, 23 in Japan, and others in locations such as Chamonix, the French ski resort."[97] But it doesn't stop there. Business for the sake of business and no higher purpose, as we have seen, has the potential to render catastrophic results in more ways than one. Instead, Patagonia is "in business to save our home planet." This statement ties the daily operations of the company into a greater cause by establishing its purpose as a force for global good while also acknowledging a broader responsibility, not only to the long-term health of the environment specifically, but to "our home planet," including all of humanity's short- and long-term afflictions.

---

97 Marisa Meltzer, "Patagonia and The North Face: Saving the World – One Puffer Jacket at a Time," The Guardian (Guardian News and Media, March 7, 2017), https://www.theguardian.com/business/2017/mar/07/the-north-face-patagonia-saving-world-one-puffer-jacket-at-a-time.

This makes it sound as though Patagonia may be trying to do more good than a single company can handle. Yet, as overly ambitious as this new statement seems, Vincent explained that "the first mission statement, adopted 27 years ago, was [also] highly aspirational at the beginning. We had not yet helped develop recycled polyester or switched to organic cotton, did not yet take every product back for recycling, had not committed to becoming carbon neutral. But over the years that mission statement became embedded in everyone's daily work life. And over the years the environmental crisis has grown more serious. The change in mission statement reflects that and our renewed commitment to the highest possible purpose." In other words, when the company started out, its original business statement, which in retrospect seems relatively narrow in focus, was indeed a bold mark for the nascent company to achieve. Now that it has grown and matured over several decades, though, so too have many of the world's problems. Patagonia has proven it's ready to take on a greater responsibility in solving those problems, so it has set a higher goal for itself, more deeply ingrained in the company's culture.

Patagonia's success directly defies the notion that social responsibility should be viewed primarily as a means to a financial end. In fact, in Vincent's eyes, "the biggest drag on responsible business practices is the emphasis placed in publicly traded companies on shareholder return as the sole legitimate goal of business." Although it may seem blasphemous to many in the business world, instead of thinking exclusively about *financial outcomes for shareholders*, we should instead focus on *overall outcomes for all stakeholders*. This request is daunting for any business, especially an international one that comes into various forms of contact with countless stakeholders all over the world and still has a bottom line to meet. But Patagonia has proven it's possible.

The key to making it all work, as other international, socially responsible companies have also discovered, is to *stop treating the financial objectives of a business as distinct from its social objectives*. The example set by Patagonia reinforces the idea that the more closely these two missions are bound to one another, the more likely a company is to succeed in achieving them both. As Vincent described, the traditional understanding of corporate social responsibility is not the most effective approach: "We agree with those who find the usual concept of 'CSR' inadequate to the current need. Responsibility should be at the heart of a business, not an ancillary effort." To regard CSR as something distinct from the core purpose of the company is to imply it is a superfluous function that can and should be sacrificed in the name of short-term profitability whenever possible. If every private actor understands social responsibility as a dispensable element secondary to personal gain, society might as well eschew the concept of individual morality entirely.

Instead, as Vincent explained, "In a time of social and environmental crisis every business should be responsible in its products, services and operations: they should do some social and environmental good and ideally help solve or begin to help solve one of our 'wicked problems.' Moreover, every business should act as best it can in the interests of all its stakeholders (employees, customers, communities, financial and environmental health)." The philosophy that collective problems demand exclusively collective solutions is imprudent. If every business forgoes its social responsibility with this thought process in mind, the world will suffer from endless buck-passing, each firm ignoring the social woes it contributes to in the hope that someone else will take care of it. But we cannot leave all our problems to be solved by another person, at another time, in another place.

International trade has brought people across the world together for mutual benefit for centuries, and there is no greater collective problem-solver than the endlessly innovating, optimizing, growing free market. The market is heavily rooted in self-preservation—but also in self-sufficiency.

In the words of the prominent libertarian philosopher Ayn Rand, "Life is a process of self-sustaining and self-generated action. If an organism fails in that action, it dies. ... It is only the concept of 'Life' that makes the concept of 'Value' possible. It is only to a living entity that things can be good or evil." Businesses exist to create value through their individual actions, but there can be no value without humanity. The concept of value is meaningless without it. Therefore, each individual action by a business must also take into consideration its effect on life, the source of the very value that sustains the enterprise itself. If we each do not work to solve the problems we contribute to, no one will do it for us. As Vincent declared, "every business must hold itself responsible for the harm to people and our planet done within the supply chain."

This last issue is of particular relevance to clothing companies like Patagonia, which rely heavily on global supply chains to manufacture their products. In 2018, Aruna Kashyap, senior counsel for the women's rights division of the Human Rights Watch (HRW) reported on the potential for massive irresponsibility in this global industry:

> *More than five years have passed since a series of deadly fire and building accidents in Pakistan and Bangladesh together killed more than 1,500 workers and injured thousands more.*

> *In the aftermath of these disasters, labor advocates ploughed through debris and dead bodies or interviewed traumatized workers to get them to recall brand names. That image underscored just how*

woefully inadequate apparel brands' approach to worker rights had been.

Five years later, we still need more information about the brands that workers produce for, to ensure that workers' rights are respected, and their safety protected.

Brand-label information matters not just for fire and building safety. The $2.4 trillion apparel industry, which predominantly employs women as garment workers, witnesses a host of labor abuses. These range from poor wages to factory owners and managers denying paid maternity benefits or even firing pregnant workers to harassment of union leaders to forced overtime work to workplace sexual harassment.[98]

In instances like these, transparency can be crucial to international corporate social responsibility—hence Patagonia's aforementioned affiliation with the Fair Labor Association. When dealing with crises that occur in different countries with weak regulatory institutions thousands of miles away, it can be difficult to hold companies accountable for labor abuses.

---

98 Aruna Kashyap, "When Clothing Labels Are a Matter of Life or Death," Human Rights Watch Women's Rights Division (The Daily Beast, May 2, 2018), https://www.hrw.org/news/2018/05/02/when-clothing-labels-are-matter-life-or-death.

NGOs like HRW can be important allies to socially responsible businesses caught in predicaments like those described
above, because they can also operate across multiple borders
to provide third-party verification of accountability. In 2017,
HRW got seventeen major apparel brands to sign a transparency pledge, agreeing to disclose which factories manufacture their goods to prevent future tragedies.[99] Patagonia, as
well as major competitors including Nike and Adidas, was
among the seventeen to commit fully to HRW's terms.[100]
Patagonia's willingness to cooperate with NGOs has no doubt
helped it overcome the challenge of transparency associated
with international CSR.

To a certain degree, compliance with nongovernmental organizations is optional for multinational companies. Obeying
the governments of the countries they operate in, on the
other hand, remains obligatory. However, Patagonia is also
challenging the assumption that companies must avoid taking action on government policies they disagree with. From
giving away the money it has saved due to recent tax cuts
to its movement to protect public lands from the Trump
administration, Patagonia has been seen by some outside

---

99   "17 Align With Transparency Pledge; Others Should Catch Up,"
      More Brands Should Reveal Where Their Clothes are Made (Human
      Rights Watch, April 20, 2017), https://www.hrw.org/news/2017/04/20/
      more-brands-should-reveal-where-their-clothes-are-made.
100 Ibid.

observers as becoming increasingly political. Do politics have any place in CSR?

Vincent seemed to think so, stating, "We are increasingly political, but our defense of public lands is also directly related to our core business as an outdoor clothing supplier. We have been giving 1 percent of sales to grassroots environmental organizations since 1985 and have strong relationships with the environmental community. These issues are close to the bone for us. Ordinarily we would regard ourselves as a part of civil society rather than political agents but with the Trump administration simply defending civil society and institutions has become a matter of politics." International companies are, by nature, highly visible. Given the risk of alienating stakeholders, this stance seems bold for such a business. But global leaders in social responsibility are also necessarily disruptors in their innovation. Why work to uphold the status quo today when you are actively trying to change the status quo for tomorrow because it contradicts your values? For Patagonia, its business is the embodiment of its values, and the latter cannot be compromised in favor of the former, otherwise it is no different from any other company.

Vincent left me with the following parting words of wisdom on the role we all share in international corporate social responsibility: "Don't fall for the myth that doing the right thing is for after six o'clock or what you tell your kids after you get off work. Over the next half-century, the resources of business, as well as government and NGOs, will be necessary to help restore human communities and our home planet to health."

[i   We will discuss such companies later, including fast food, tobacco, and alcohol.

PART III

BUILDING
A BETTER
FUTURE

CHAPTER 6

SOCIALLY RESPONSIBLE INVESTING (SRI)

Much of the dialogue on international CSR often overlooks an irreplaceable aspect to conscientious enterprise: the role of investors. Without the flow of capital into socially responsible companies, they cannot exist. But just how crucial are the social motivations of investors in helping businesses build a better world?

In recent years, firms have emerged centered precisely on the principle that global investors, like companies, can do well by doing good. One such investor, billionaire Paul Tudor Jones, founder of the Robin Hood Foundation, a New York-based poverty reduction and disaster relief charity, is among those championing the power of finance as a force for global good. In 2013, Jones founded JUST Capital, a nonprofit with the goal of creating a more ethical marketplace by helping Americans find companies whose social priorities match their own so they can align their financial interests with their charitable ones.

The clearest way to build a better future for the world, in Jones' eyes, is through private enterprise. "There's a $19 trillion private economy," he said. "It's four times the size of the public sector. It's 40 times the size of the philanthropic sector. If we're going to have true social change, it's going to come through the private sector."[101] If socially responsible businesses are the most influential drivers of human progress, however, the general public must engage with them. Otherwise, without the flow of capital from more and more stakeholders, these companies will be powerless to bring about the change they seek—which is why skeptics of capitalism in recent years have prevented significant social progress from taking place. "Five years ago, it was apparent even then, I think, that capitalism needed to be modernized," Jones argues. "I just saw this poll — 51 percent of millennials from 18 to 29 either don't believe or [are] opposed to

101 Lizzy Gurdus, "Paul Tudor Jones: The $19 Trillion Private Sector Should Lead Social Change," CNBC (CNBC, November 2, 2018), https://www.cnbc.com/2018/11/02/paul-tudor-jones-the-private-sector-can-lead-social-change.html.

capitalism."[102] It's clear, then, that the private sector must innovate to increase its capacity for social justice.

That's where JUST Capital comes in, and its effects have proven beneficial socially as well as financially. The JUST index of ethical companies has surpassed the broader market in each of the last seven quarters, outperforming the 1,000 largest companies (known in the finance world as the Russell 1000) by 3.9 percent overall since its founding.[103] Moreover, since 2007, the current index, which includes such international companies as Eli Lilly, Accenture, Clorox, and Ingersoll-Rand, has outperformed the Russell 1000 by nearly 50 percent.[104] Focusing on businesses with strong values, then, can be a true boon for investors in more ways than one.

But why do socially conscious companies tend to outperform the market? The most important factors in determining whether a company is just, according to Tudor's system, are worker compensation and treatment.[105] High achievement in these areas attracts the most effective employees, who create the best products, which in turn yield the highest stock prices. This is especially relevant to multinational companies. The use of global supply chains creates the potential for workers

---

102 Ibid.
103 Ibid.
104 Ibid.
105 Ibid.

halfway across the world to be brutalized and underpaid to generate shoddy products. But, if Jones' evidently successful theory of investing holds any broader significance, it may indicate that these companies can do better business by taking better care of their workers and selling better products, ultimately generating a greater profit.

Yet this philosophy has not caught on with all investors. In fact, some have adopted the exact opposite approach. One example of this can be found in USA Mutuals' Barrier Fund (VICEX), formerly known as the Barrier Fund, essentially the moral opposite of JUST Capital. Investors in the Barrier Fund profit from ownership of so-called "sin stocks"—shares in companies that purvey alcohol, tobacco, other legal drugs, weapons, and gambling. Subscribers to this philosophy, which is at best apathetic to the moral implications of their investments, have found substantial financial success. The Barrier Fund's portfolio manager Jordan Waldrep explained, "In the long term, vice investing makes sense because these are often well-managed companies with established brands and extremely loyal customers."[106] No matter what the rest of the market is doing, smokers, drinkers, and gamblers will continue to engage in self-destructive habits, yielding

---

106 John Daly, "Vice Fund Tempted by More than Tobacco and Booze," Irish Examiner (Irishexaminer.com, August 7, 2018), https://www.irishexaminer.com/breakingnews/business/vice-fund-tempted-by-more-than-tobacco-and-booze-860446.html.

consistent returns for investors. The guarantee of continued consumption of these products offers investors a higher degree of certainty than do many other stocks. Furthermore, because morally responsible investors avoid owning sin stocks, they are often undervalued, creating an opportunity for less socially conscious individuals to acquire them at low prices despite the relatively low risk associated with them.

While this makes sin stocks especially attractive to investors more concerned about making a quick buck than improving the world, a more compelling case can still be made for investing in socially conscious companies. In its first fifteen years of existence, the Barrier Fund outperformed the S&P 500 by roughly 1.6 percent per year.[107] While these returns are impressive, they don't quite stack up to the JUST index, which has outpaced the S&P 500 by 3.4 percent since its inception, bringing in for its investors more than double the returns of the Barrier Fund.[108] This is more than just one isolated case. In fact, writing for the *Harvard Business Review*, Ravi Venkatesan and Leslie Benton pointed out, "According to data collected by the Ethisphere Institute, companies that implement effective [CSR] programs realize a 10.72% 'Ethics Premium.' Research also demonstrates that ethical companies have lower turnover among employees. And consumers

---

107 Ibid.
108 Gurdus, "Paul Tudor Jones."

are placing a higher and higher value on whether a company has ethical practices, too."[109] In other words, we have strong reason to believe ethical behavior makes companies more valuable in several different ways. It follows, then, that investors can gain more from devoting their capital to the world's socially responsible businesses than they can from investing in socially corrosive companies.

What implications, if any, does this have for global progress? One prominent investor with financial interests around the globe, *Mad Money* host Jim Cramer, remains a vocal proponent of trading sin stocks regardless of what they represent because the only commandment of investing is "Thou shalt make money."[110] Some even justify sin stocks by suggesting you use the returns from those investments to support socially responsible causes. Writing for *AOL*, Brian Lund explained, "When you avoid buying a sin stock it doesn't affect the company in question and ultimately is an empty gesture. Instead, why not 'use' those sin stocks and create some good? A strategy that—when warranted—takes advantage of their earnings power and historical performance can be a way to improve your profits, which you can then take a portion of and donate to charities or causes you believe

---

109 Venkatesan and Benton, "How Companies Can Take a Stand Against Bribery."

110 "Cramer's 'Mad Money' Recap: Sin Stocks," TheStreet (TheStreet, August 30, 2006), https://www.thestreet.com/story/10306493/1/cramers-mad-money-recap-sin-stocks.html.

in."[111] On the surface, this appears to dismantle the connection between CSR and socially responsible investing (SRI).

Professor Theo Vermaelen also contended that investors can reconcile any discrepancies between their personal values and investment portfolio by donating the profits of sin stocks to charity. He offered as an example someone who invested $5,000 in the arms manufacturer Smith & Wesson. From January 2012 to June 2016, "S&W's stock price has increased by 433 percent from US$4.50 to US$24, largely as a result of terrorist attacks and gun owners' fears that U.S. President Barack Obama would take away their guns. The socially responsible investor could then use his profits (US$21,650) to donate to a group that lobbies against the National Rifle Association."[112] This approach, however, neglects several important aspects of socially responsible investing.

First of all, it would be self-defeating for an investor to own stock in companies that they do not patronize and actively try to deter others from patronizing. This is especially true when that investor's ultimate intention is to devote the profits from those stocks to other businesses or causes actively

---

111 Brian Lund, "Why Even the Righteous Should Invest in Sin," AOL. com (AOL, September 19, 2014), https://www.aol.com/article/finance/2014/09/19/sin-stocks-good-investments/20962595/.

112 Theo Vermaelen, "Doing Good by Investing in Sin," INSEAD Knowledge (Institut Européen d'Administration des Affaires, June 30, 2016), https://knowledge.insead.edu/blog/insead-blog/doing-good-by-investing-in-sin-4774.

seeking to undermine the continued success of those stocks. A nondrinker can own stock in Anheuser-Busch, but if he discourages his family and friends from drinking and uses his own money to buy responsibly sourced juice, he makes the juice company more profitable and does nothing to support the alcohol stock he owns. His personal financial behavior, informed by his ethics, is incongruent with his dispassionate investment strategy. Similarly, a proponent of gun control can own stock in Smith & Wesson, but not owning a gun means not supporting the value of that stock, and devoting his returns from that stock to the promotion of gun control actively damages its value. Because of this dilemma, holding shares in a company you deem unethical works against your own interests.

There is still the argument that not investing in unethical companies is an ineffective way to combat their irresponsible practices. But suppose we have a highly valued multinational corporation whose actions are morally reprehensible—say, using child laborers to chop down rainforests to create a highly addictive, deadly product. We'll call this company Vandelay Industries (VNDL). SRI skeptics like Cramer and Lund are correct in their assertion that when you invest in Vandelay Industries, you purchase shares not from the evil corporation itself but rather from other investors. Vandelay doesn't get any of the money used to purchase its shares. However, this transaction then sustains the high price of those shares. Demand for owning part of an unethical company keeps that company valuable and robust. If people decide to stop buying shares of Vandelay, the reduced demand would cause the share price, and thus the value of the company as a whole, to nosedive. This outcome would be catastrophic for Vandelay, which would be forced either to change its immoral practices to attract new investors, increasing demand and raising its share price, or to suffer serious consequences. A depreciating share price would make it more difficult for Vandelay to acquire credit, entice more investors, and form valuable partnerships. The morale of employees who own stock in the company may also diminish, and if the share price tumbles too low, Vandelay may need to reverse-split its shares or even go private, which is what happened to Playboy between 2009 and 2011.[113], [114] An investor, by not purchasing shares of Vandelay, plays a small role in denying the company crucial support.

While an individual cannot singlehandedly bring down a multinational corporation like Vandelay, their decision not to invest in it can be part of a larger force for global good, just as one person conserving energy cannot reverse climate change, but many people choosing to conserve energy can lessen the

113 "Hugh Hefner Sells LA Property as Financial Crisis Hits Playboy," The Telegraph (Telegraph Media Group, August 11, 2009), https://www.telegraph.co.uk/finance/recession/6007514/Hugh-Hefner-sells-LA-property-as-financial-crisis-hits-Playboy.html.

114 "Hefner's Playboy Buyout Seen Closing Friday As Tender Minimum Met," Dow Jones Newswire (Wall Street Journal, March 4, 2011), http://online.wsj.com/article/BT-CO-20110304-708619.html.

climate crisis's effects. The market is based on aggregate decisions of countless individuals. If millions of people, on the individual level, demand social responsibility, they can create it on a global scale. Regardless of who is selling stock in Vandelay, to purchase it is to tacitly endorse it. When many people want to purchase that stock, they create demand that keeps Vandelay healthy and support for its environment-ravaging, child-manipulating, consumer-killing operations.

And, even if an investor is still more concerned with long-run personal financial returns than long-run global social outcomes, it may be worth putting capital into the highly profitable companies that make up the JUST index. Alternatively, it may be prudent to invest in socially responsible exchange-traded funds (ETFs) like DSI by BlackRock iShares, which has yielded an average annual return of 8.11 percent since its inception in 2006.[i] But perhaps the most persuasive evidence of SRI's profitability comes from 2016 research by Deutsche Bank and the University of Hamburg. With aggregated empirical data from over 2,000 different studies, researchers found an extremely positive correlation between the integration of environmental, social, and governance (ESG) criteria into the investment process and corporate financial performance.[115]

---

115 Gunnar Friede, Timo Busch, and Alexander Bassen, "ESG and Financial Performance: Aggregated Evidence from More than 2000 Empirical Studies," Journal of Sustainable Finance and Investment (Deutsche Bank Asset Management and University of Hamburg, January 14, 2016), https://www.db.com/

The below graphs indicate that most studies found a positive correlation between ESG criteria and corporate financial performance, regardless of geographic region, asset classes, and which aspect of ESG a company focused on.

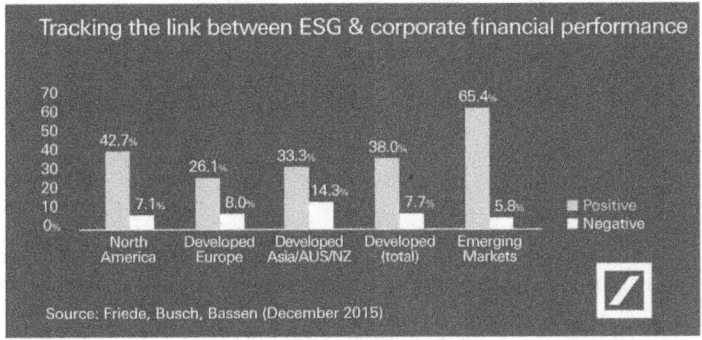

116

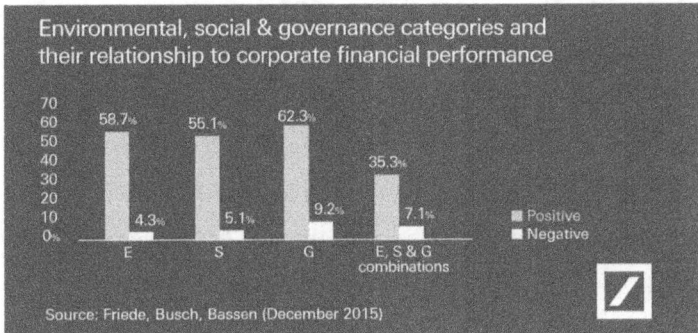

117

newsroom_news/2016/ghp/esg-and-financial-performance-aggregat-ed-evidence-from-more-than-200-empirical-studies-en-11363.htm.
116 Ibid.
117 Ibid.

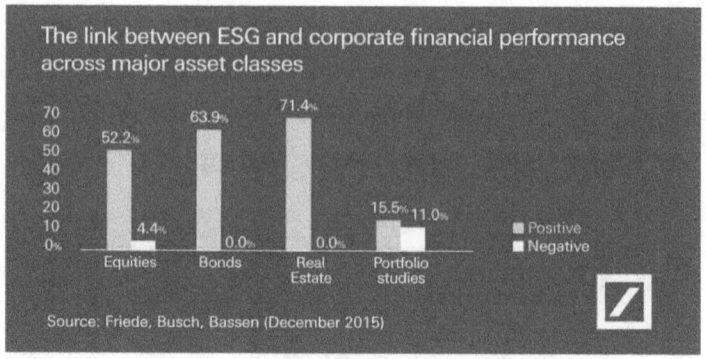

The link between ESG and corporate financial performance across major asset classes

Source: Friede, Busch, Bassen (December 2015)

118

Many prominent investors have become advocates for investing in socially responsible businesses, including billionaire former hedge fund manager Tom Steyer, who decided to divest from carbon-polluting companies in 2012.[119] Erika Karp, founder of the $1 billion SRI firm Cornerstone Capital Group, points out that "all investing has an impact. ... We are seeing a transformation of traditional philanthropy strategies towards impact investing, which makes sense. But ultimately, we're going to move even further towards market return investing with social impact."[120] Steyer and Karp are not outliers. The Forum for Sustainable and Responsible

---

118 Ibid.

119 Michael Barbaro and Coral Davenport, "Aims of Donor Are Shadowed by Past in Coal," The New York Times (The New York Times, July 4, 2014), https://www.nytimes.com/2014/07/05/us/politics/prominent-environmentalist-helped-fund-coal-projects.html.

120 Amy Bennett, "The Economics of Sustainable and Impact Investing," Real Leaders (Real Leaders, May 7, 2018), https://real-leaders.com/the-economics-of-sustainable-and-impact-investing/.

Investment estimates that over 200 institutions and money managers controlled a total of $6.57 trillion in assets at the beginning of 2014, an increase of 76 percent from just two years prior.[121] The amount of money flowing into ethical enterprises is rapidly increasing, which means that we can only expect the number, size, and impact of socially responsible international companies to grow in the coming years.

Not all well-intentioned investors hit their mark in supporting international CSR, though. For example, as a way of combating global poverty, Muhammad Yunus founded the Grameen Bank and pioneered the concept of microfinance, or the disbursing of small loans to impoverished entrepreneurs around the world who would not otherwise qualify for loans from traditional banks. Originally, this seemed like such a promising idea that Yunus even won a Nobel Prize for it. However, instead of addressing the systemic issues causing poverty, it exacerbates them, because in some countries over 90 percent of microfinance use goes toward consumption rather than building businesses.[122] As anthropologist Jason Hickel pointed out, this means that "borrowers don't generate

---

121 "Report on US Sustainable, Responsible, and Impact Investing Trends 2014," The Forum for Responsible and Sustainable Investment (USSIF Foundation and Bloomberg, 2014), https://www.ussif.org/Files/Publications/SIF_Trends_14.F.ES.pdf.

122 Jason Hickel, "The Microfinance Delusion: Who Really Wins?," The Guardian (Guardian News and Media, June 10, 2015), https://www.theguardian.com/global-development-professionals-network/2015/jun/10/the-microfinance-delusion-who-really-wins.

any new income that they can use to repay their loans so they end up taking out new loans to repay the old ones, wrapping themselves in layers of debt. … The only consistent winners in the microfinance game are the lenders, many of whom charge exorbitant interest rates that sometimes reach up to 200% per annum. In the past we would have called such people loan sharks, but today they're called microfinance providers."[123] While microfinance initially seemed like a promising method to alleviate global poverty, it has since proven unsuccessful in this regard.

Some posit, just as David Hulme, Joseph Hanlon, and Armando Barrientos do in the title of their book, that it would be more beneficial to *Just Give Money to the Poor*.[124] However, this method is unsustainable for investors who need to receive some return on their investment—which leads us to conclude that SRI is likely more effective when aimed at socially responsible international businesses. Instead of simply giving their money away or funding manipulative microfinance providers, investors looking to make a difference for impoverished people around the world are better off backing businesses that can lift people in developing countries out

---

123 Ibid.

124 David Hulme, Joseph Hanlon, and Armando Barrientos, "Just Give Money to the Poor: The Development Revolution from the Global South" (Kumarian Press, 2012), https://books.google.co.za/books/about/Just_Give_Money_to_the_Poor.html?id=M2WWHIzQONoC&hl=en.

of poverty by offering them careers with decent wages and fair treatment.

Prominent investors around the world are developing new strategies to devote more capital to this cause. For example, former JPMorgan Managing Director John Fullerton founded the Capital Institute, a nonpartisan think tank that published a guide on investing in what it calls "a regenerative economy." The Capital Institute seeks to overcome challenges associated with "the misguided ascent of 'shareholder wealth maximisation' (at the expense of all other stakeholder interests) [and] the well-intended but equally misguided practice of using stock-based incentives, and stock options in particular, as the dominant form of senior management compensation, which incentivises them to focus only on short-term results at the expense of the long-term health of the enterprise, people and planet."[125] Even RBC, Canada's largest bank, is adjusting its metrics to focus more on the social impact of its investments in socially responsible businesses.

Valerie Chort, RBC's vice president of corporate citizenship, and Hamoon Ekhtiari, CEO of Audacious Futures, wrote, "Traditionally, most of our measurement efforts

---

125 John Fullerton, "Six Reasons Why Our Stock Markets Are No Longer Fit for Purpose," The Guardian (Guardian News and Media, October 21, 2013), https://www.theguardian.com/sustainable-business/stock-markets-no-longer-fit-purpose.

were customized for each funded program and primarily focused on input and output numbers such as dollars spent, number of participants, and number of organizations supported. That approach, however, made it difficult to measure the impact of our programs on participants."[126] To this end, RBC created a new tool called the Impact Measurement Framework (IMF), which quantifies the social outcomes of their work, including "the social economic, environmental, employee, business, and brand impact of our initiatives and investments. The IMF provides a consistent way of measuring our initiatives and investments across our portfolio and a more meaningful view of our holistic impact," Chort and Ekhtiari elaborated.[127] But they did not stop there. RBC's social initiatives have a global reach, and international problems demand international solutions. "To ensure that the IMF is aligned with other commonly accepted frameworks, we drew on global reporting guidance, including the Sustainable Development Goals. ... We believe that RBC's mind-set shift and emerging approach has great potential—particularly for purpose-led organizations. Purpose instills strategic clarity, channels innovation, drives transformation, unites people, and builds bridges. Making CSR core to

---

126 Valerie Chort and Hamoon Ekhtiari, "A New Model for CSR (SSIR)," Stanford Social Innovation Review (Stanford University, 2018), https://ssir.org/articles/entry/a_new_model_for_csr.

127 Ibid.

your organization's purpose will lead to transformational change and social impact."[128]

RBC is not alone in its commitment to international CSR. Bank of America has indirectly created 13,000 jobs by providing support and mentorship for hundreds of female entrepreneurs in Afghanistan and Rwanda.[129] Where microfinance has failed in empowering entrepreneurs to alleviate global poverty, traditional lending institutions have succeeded by developing a renewed focus on international CSR.

SRI has taken on many forms, large and small in scope. The most important takeaway, though, is that conscious investing can be both highly profitable on the financial end and highly impactful on the social end. A business cannot operate without capital. While shrugged off by some as irrelevant, recent innovations in SRI have produced a measurable impact on socially responsible businesses around the world, and they will undoubtedly continue to play a tremendous role in the future of international CSR.

[i]   As of Dec. 25, 2018, per https://www.ishares.com/us/products/239667/ishares-msci-kld-400-social-etf

128 Ibid.
129 "Bank of America and IEEW: Investing in Women Leaders from Afghanistan and Rwanda," About Bank of America (Bank of America, May 6, 2016), https://about.bankofamerica.com/en-us/partnering-locally/boa-ieew-partnership.html#fbid=arR-cEe6X85.

CHAPTER 7

CSR CHALLENGES POSED BY AUTOMATION AND TECHNOLOGY

AUTOMATION: NOT NECESSARILY IRRESPONSIBLE

"ROBOTS WILL TAKE OUR JOBS," declare anxiety-inducing headlines from several[130] major[131] news[132]

---

130 Larry Elliott, "Robots Will Take Our Jobs. We'd Better Plan Now, before It's Too Late | Larry Elliott," The Guardian (Guardian News and Media, February 1, 2018), https://www.theguardian.com/commentisfree/2018/feb/01/robots-take-our-jobs-amazon-go-seattle.

131 Blake Morgan, "Robots Will Take Our Jobs And We Need A Plan: 4 Scenarios For The Future," Forbes (Forbes Magazine, September 7, 2018), https://www.forbes.com/sites/blakemorgan/2018/09/05/robots-will-take-our-jobs-and-we-need-a-plan-4-scenarios-for-the-future/.

132 Niall Firth, "This Time Robots Really Are Going to Take Our Jobs," Slate Magazine (Slate, May 4, 2014), https://slate.com/

sources.[133] Trepidation about the rise of machines pervades the business world. ATKearney's most recent annual survey of global business executives revealed that technological risks were one of their foremost concerns for the year ahead, second only to political risk. Interestingly, the results showed that "adopting new technologies is the only issue area that emerges as both a top opportunity and a top challenge in business operations."[134] This finding is unsurprising given the tremendous role that recent, rapid technological advances have played in the expansion of globalization and, with it, the development of international companies into what they are today. Still, many cannot shake the fear that robots are on track to replace human beings in the workplace. While this isn't exactly the case—more on that momentarily—emerging technologies in the coming years will present companies with numerous major ethical challenges, perhaps the greatest of which is the threat these technologies pose to the international labor market.

technology/2014/05/robots-taking-jobs-technology-will-re-place-driving-routine-physical-labor-information-processing.html.

133 Stephen Marche, "Everybody Knows Robots Will Take Our Jobs, But We Can't Admit It. Why?," Esquire (Esquire, October 11, 2017), https://www.esquire.com/news-politics/news/a42876/millennial-financial-crisis-technology/.

134 Paul A. Laudicina, Courtney Rickert McCaffrey, and Erik R. Peterson, "Rising to the Challenge: 2018 Views from the C-Suite," An Annual Survey of Global Business Executives (A. T. Kearney Global Business Policy Council, 2018), https://www.atkearney.com/web/global-business-policy-council/views-from-the-c-suite/.

In 2018, Pew Research Center polled thousands of adults in ten countries spanning various levels of economic development, seeking their input on the effects workplace automation will have on their economies. A majority in nine of the ten countries surveyed believe that governments, schools, and individuals themselves share most of the onus to retrain personnel in preparation for the impending penetration of robots into the workplace, ranking employers as the ones with the least responsibility to do so.[135] Researchers Richard Wike and Bruce Stokes noted in their analysis of the data that "profit maximization, and the relatively high cost of human labor, helps drive automation. The average hourly cost of a manufacturing worker is $49 in Germany and $36 in the U.S. The hourly cost of a robot is $4... In all 10 advanced and emerging economies polled, large majorities say that in the next 50 years robots and computers will probably or definitely do much of the work currently done by humans."[136] Moreover, they alleged that the takeover of machines is already underway in certain sectors of some countries' economies. Companies in South Korea, for example, have already installed over 600 industrial robots per 10,000

---

135 Richard Wike and Bruce Stokes, "In Advanced and Emerging Economies Alike, Worries About Job Automation," Pew Research Center's Global Attitudes Project (Pew Research Center's Global Attitudes Project, September 20, 2018), http://www.pewglobal.org/2018/09/13/in-advanced-and-emerging-economies-alike-worries-about-job-automation/.

136 Ibid.

manufacturing workers, compared with over 300 in Japan and just under 200 in the United States.[137]

The most glaring implication of this study for socially conscious international companies is that the rise of automation forces management to choose between the conflicting interests of different groups of stakeholders: they must either cut costs by replacing human labor with machine labor to boost profits and support the interests of corporate owners and investors, or they must preserve the livelihood of their workers by retaining them even though doing so would be more costly. Regardless of how socially responsible a company is, the latter option is untenable because it makes the company less competitive than it could be. Any company that does not take advantage of the best technologies available to maximize efficiency and minimize costs will not be able to sustain itself for long.

When viewed through the appropriate lens, however, this situation does not present the CSR dilemma it appears to. Automation in the workplace is too often thought of as a zero-sum game, but that's not actually the case. As Cisco's chief executive for the U.K. and Ireland, Scot Gardner, said, "I don't buy the idea that there are 100 jobs, and if you automate 40, there are 60 left. I don't think the economy works like that.

---

137 Ibid.

Markets adapt to the conditions they have."[138] While the researchers in this study are correct in their assertion that the hourly costs of human labor in developed countries are much greater than those of robots, the two are not mutually exclusive. On the contrary, there is a substantial body of evidence to suggest that companies benefit most not by replacing workers with robots but by introducing technologies that make those workers more efficient.

McDonald's—despite its shortcomings in other areas of CSR—has proven that international companies can implement emerging technologies to fulfill their obligations to all stakeholders by retaining its workers *and* increasing profits for its investors. Its decision to introduce interactive self-service kiosks has drawn criticism, including from former CEO of McDonald's USA, Ed Rensi, for its purported effect on employment.[139] "There is no evidence, however, that any of these efforts are leading to overall reductions in labor," Jonathan Maze of *Nation's Restaurant News* declared. "Restaurants' labor costs increased in 2016. They continued to increase so far in 2017. And the industry has added about

---

138 Alex Scroxton, "Automation and CSR Are Driving Reskilling Process for UK Plc, Says Cisco," ComputerWeekly.com, November 6, 2018, https://www.computerweekly.com/news/252452041/Automation-and-CSR-are-driving-reskilling-process-for-UK-plc-says-Cisco.

139 Ed Rensi, "McDonald's Says Goodbye Cashiers, Hello Kiosks," orbes (Forbes Magazine, July 11, 2018), https://www.forbes.com/sites/edrensi/2018/07/11/mcdonalds-says-goodbye-cashiers-hello-kiosks/#3b2a786d6f14.

273,000 employees over the past 12 months, according to federal data, a rate higher than that of the overall economy."[140] The company will, after all, need staff to assist customers with the kiosks, prepare and serve the food, and clean and maintain the restaurants; with increased business from the kiosks, the company will need more staff to carry out each of these tasks.

The company, which aims to install kiosks at 14,000 branches worldwide by 2020, has seen a 5–6 percent increase in sales in the first year following its installation at each branch.[141] The financial benefits may be even greater than this, though. The *Harvard Business Review* highlighted one branch where, following the installation of kiosks, "the average check size was a dollar higher — a 30% increase at the time. And they found that 20% of customers who didn't initially order a drink would buy one when it was offered. Kiosks, of course, never forget to upsell. In addition to all of this, there is some research from 2011 showing that a seven-second reduction in service times in fast food restaurants can increase the company's market share by 1% to 3%."[142] Kiosks also benefit custom-

---

140 Jonathan Maze, "Kiosks Are No Labor Savior," On the Margin (Nation's Restaurant News, June 26, 2017), https://www.nrn.com/operations/kiosks-are-no-labor-savior.

141 Mike Pomranz, "Self-Serve Kiosks May Not Be Killing Fast Food Jobs After All," Food & Wine, June 26, 2017, https://www.foodandwine.com/news/self-serve-kiosks-may-not-be-killing-fast-food-jobs-after-all.

142 Gretchen Gavett, "How Self-Service Kiosks Are Changing Customer Behavior," Harvard Business Review (Harvard

ers by improving order accuracy, increasing convenience, and shortening wait times, all of which benefit customers and, by extension, the business as a whole, which will earn more profits to reinvest in expanding the business by hiring more employees.

McDonald's isn't the only international company that can use emerging technologies to benefit all stakeholders. After rolling out its own kiosks, mobile ordering, and electronic payment, Panera Bread found in its 2015 second-quarter earnings report that, even though it had decreased input labor, it had increased labor hours to account for the additional demand resulting from the new digital interface.[143] Although workers were no longer necessary for taking all of the orders, the use of these technologies increased the volume of orders and thus the need for employees elsewhere in the business. Panera still needed them to provide customer service, staff the counter for those who chose to order in person, prepare and deliver orders to customers, and tend to miscellaneous back-of-house duties.

University, March 11, 2015), https://hbr.org/2015/03/how-self-service-kiosks-are-changing-customer-behavior.

143 "Panera Bread (PNRA) Ronald M. Shaich on Q2 2015 Results - Earnings Call Transcript," Seeking Alpha (Panera Bread, July 29, 2015), https://seekingalpha.com/article/3370365-panera-bread-pnra-ronald-m-shaich-on-q2-2015-results-earnings-call-transcript?part=single.

A joint study by the Rotman School of Management, Duke's Fuqua School of Business, and the National University of Singapore found that companies that implement self-service technologies effectively circumvent "social friction," or the anxiety a customer experiences about the way an employee may perceive them when ordering in person.[144] When customers interact directly with another human being, they risk being judged or misunderstood, which deters them from placing complicated or unhealthy orders and thus cuts into the company's potential profit and leaves the customer dissatisfied—but technology can be used to sidestep such social inhibitions.[145] This method helps customers freely order what they want, improving the consumer experience for the benefit of stakeholders both within the company and outside of it, which demonstrates that companies can implement new technologies in a socially responsible way, to the mutual advantage of customers, workers, and investors.

But the above examples come from the service sector. What about the millions of manufacturing jobs that robots are taking over from human workers? The World Bank calculated that the total population of the United States skyrocketed

---

144 Avi Goldfarb et al., "The Effect of Social Interaction on Economic Transactions: Evidence from Changes in Two Retail Formats," rotman.utoronto.ca (University of Toronto Rotman School of Management, June 2014), http://www-2.rotman.utoronto.ca/~agoldfarb/socialtransactions.pdf.

145 Ibid.

by over 129 million between 1965 and 2016,[146] but based on data from the Bureau of Labor Statistics, journalist Timothy B. Lee estimated that the number of Americans working in industries that manufacture goods *declined* by about one million over that same time period.[147] "Declining manufacturing employment over the past 30 years has given a lot of people the impression that America's manufacturing sector is in decline. But that's actually wrong," Lee explained in an article for Vox. "American factories are about twice as efficient today as they were three decades ago. So we're producing more and more stuff, even as we use fewer and fewer people to do it."[148] If there are fewer people working in the manufacturing sector, but more goods are being produced then, naturally, robots must be the ones doing the manufacturing. This reasoning, however, can be somewhat misleading.

The truth is not that robots *took away* these jobs from humans. In reality, the rise of machines in manufacturing is a consequence, not a cause, of humans vacating positions in that sector. In other words, humans are leaving manufacturing jobs for a variety of other reasons, such as younger

---

146 "Total U.S. Population," World Bank Group (United Nations Population Division, 2016), https://data.worldbank.org/indicator/SP.POP.TOTL?end=2016&locations=US&start=1965.
147 Timothy B. Lee, "27 Charts That Will Change How You Think about the American Economy," Vox (Vox, October 10, 2016), https://www.vox.com/new-money/2016/10/10/12933426/27-charts-changing-economy.
148 Ibid.

generations reaching higher levels of educational attainment and thus qualifying for careers elsewhere, leaving companies with no choice but to bring in robots to remain competitive.

To demonstrate this point, I would like for a moment to step away from the international scope of this book to examine a case in my own hometown of Amesbury, Massachusetts. Today an unassuming rural community of fewer than 20,000 people, Amesbury was once home to a number of extremely prosperous industrial companies, including a large hat factory, multiple prominent carriage manufacturers, and several textile mills. Because of technological and economic changes in the twentieth century, however, all these industries declined, and manufacturing jobs disappeared from the town and its surrounding communities in the Merrimack Valley.

Yet, despite the collapse of the once-booming carriage industry, Amesbury's economy is fine. Aided by new technologies, manufacturing has since returned to towns like it throughout Massachusetts, but with a new face. John Lavoie, superintendent of Greater Lawrence Public School, a vocational school of over 1,500 students in Andover,[149] said that for every stu-

---

149 "Greater Lawrence Regional Vocational Technical School," Massachusetts School and District Profiles (Massachusetts Department of Elementary and Secondary Education), accessed December 27, 2018, http://profiles.doe.mass.edu/general/general.aspx?topNavID=1&leftNavId=100&orgcode=08230000&orgtypecode=5.

dent they put to work, they have about four job openings.[150] And this is not an isolated occurrence. In May 2018, in fact, the Institute for Supply Management predicted manufacturing employment would grow by 1.8 percent more than it had the previous year.[151]

The common narrative that productivity growth from machinery kills jobs simply doesn't match up with these facts. In some cases, in fact, the opposite seems to be true. The factor "holding back companies from purchasing equipment [is that] they don't have the workers or the skills" necessary to run the equipment, Lavoie observed.[152] Far from the notion that robots are excluding humans from manufacturing jobs, the new reality of the workplace is that workers and technology are becoming ever more interdependent. As MIT economics professor David H. Autor remarked in a paper on this topic in 2015, "Clearly, the past two centuries of automation and technological progress have not made human labor obsolete: the employment-to-population ratio rose during the 20th century even as women moved from home to market; and although the unemployment

---

150 Christine LaFave Grace, "Help (Still) Wanted: Manufacturers Struggle to Fill Open Jobs," Plant Services (Putman Media, June 14, 2018), https://www.plantservices.com/articles/2018/wf-help-still-wanted-manufacturers-struggle-to-fill-open-jobs/?show=all.

151 Ibid.

152 Ibid.

rate fluctuates cyclically, there is no apparent long-run increase."[153] Those worried about robots taking our jobs can rest assured that automation is unlikely to drive us from the workplace any time soon.

You may now be wondering why, in a book about international corporate social responsibility, I have just devoted substantial page space to a discussion on the threat of automation only to conclude that it is not a danger to employment. As we will see when we consider the role of international corporations, the growing interdependence of human and machine labor across the world means the work we do is fundamentally changing, which has its own serious consequences that companies can and must address in the short term with socially responsible practices.

THE TRUE CHALLENGE OF AUTOMATION IN INTERNATIONAL CSR

Although technology will endanger the global workforce in the coming years, it will not do so in quite the way many have speculated. International corporations rely heavily on emerging technologies to conduct their day-to-day operations. Global supply chains can't be coordinated by carrier

---

153 David H. Autor, "Why Are There Still So Many Jobs? The History and Future of Workplace Automation," economics.mit.edu (Journal of Economic Perspectives, 2015), https://economics.mit.edu/files/11563.

pigeons, after all. Developments in communications, transportation, and computing have already begun to reshape the way corporations use these supply chains by enabling them to vastly expand service exports, for example, but even more dramatic changes could be on the horizon.

Automation has taken on new forms in recent years, including 3D printing and the "internet of things," or the increasingly sophisticated network of devices that can connect and exchange information without interacting with a human. According to the International Labor Organization (ILO), these forms of automation all threaten the future of the global economy through the polarization or "hollowing out" of the global labor market.[154] In other words, through irresponsible implementation of automation, international corporations are contributing heavily to the demise of the middle class.

This phenomenon is particularly relevant to international companies because it is not isolated to any single state. Dr. Steve McIntosh explained that, throughout developed countries, "if jobs are ranked by their initial wage at a point in time in the late 1980s or early 1990s, then increases in employment

---

154 Gary Rynhart, "ASEAN in Transformation: How Technology Is Changing Jobs and Enterprises," Bureau for Employers' Activities (International Labour Organization, April 17, 2017), https://www.ilo.org/wcmsp5/groups/public/---asia/---ro-bangkok/---ilo-jakarta/documents/presentation/wcms_552346.pdf.

share are observed at the top and bottom of this distribution, whereas those jobs that were in the middle have lost employment share over time."[155] Middle-income occupations make up a smaller and smaller percent of the total labor market as time goes on. However, this hollowing out is not limited to wealthy countries. Dr. Indhira Santos of the World Bank reached a similar conclusion about the labor market in the developing world: "On the one hand, the share of employment in high-skilled, high-paying occupations (managers, professionals and technicians) and low-skilled, low-paying occupations (elementary, service, and sales workers) is growing. On the other hand, the share of employment in middle-skilled, middle-paying occupations (clerks, plant and machine operators) is being squeezed."[156] This polarization threatens to disrupt the entire global labor force.

Although automation results in increased productivity, the hollowing out of average-skilled, average-income careers could result in a thinning of the middle class, which in itself would be detrimental for humanity in more ways than one.

---

155 Steve McIntosh, "Hollowing out and the Future of the Labour Market," www.gov.uk/bis (United Kingdom Department for Business, Innovation and Skills, October 2013), https://assets.publishing.service.gov.uk/government/uploads/system/uploads/attachment_data/file/250206/bis-13-1213-hollowing-out-and-future-of-the-labour-market.pdf.

156 Indhira Santos, "Labor Market Polarization in Developing Countries: Challenges Ahead," World Bank Blogs (World Bank Group, June 10, 2016), http://blogs.worldbank.org/developmenttalk/labor-market-polarization-developing-countries-challenges-ahead.

Studies by New York University professors Adam Przeworski and William Easterly revealed that a healthy middle class is requisite for a robust democracy[157] and that "middle-class societies have more income and growth."[158] The polarization of the global labor force, then, jeopardizes political and economic progress in developing and developed countries alike. This concern results from corporations' implementation of automated technologies.

Take, for example, Southeast Asia's enormous textiles, clothing, and footwear (TCF) industry, in which robotic automation and "sewbots" threaten to displace workers.[159] Cost-reduction agreements, minimum wage increases, and consumer demand for higher-quality products, along with increased competition from regional powers like China and economic nationalist demands for the reshoring of manufacturing jobs to developed countries like the United States, all contribute to added pressure for TCF companies to automate manufacturing.[160]

---

157 Dambisa Moyo, "Why the Survival of Democracy Depends on a Strong Middle-Class," The Globe and Mail (The Globe and Mail, Inc., April 20, 2018), https://www.theglobeandmail.com/opinion/article-why-the-survival-of-democracy-depends-on-a-strong-middle-class/.

158 William Easterly, "The Middle Class Consensus and Economic Development," williameasterly.files.wordpress.com (World Bank Group, August 2010), https://williameasterly.files.wordpress.com/2010/08/34_easterly_middleclassconsensus_prp.pdf.

159 Rynhart, "ASEAN in Transformation."

160 Ibid.

Increased automation benefits highly skilled workers because it results in higher demand for their technical expertise. Meanwhile, advances in technology have enabled companies to save money by automating major aspects of traditionally middle-income occupations, decreasing the skill level required to do these jobs, and electronically outsourcing them to low-wage workers. As a result, it remains more efficient to employ human beings to do some jobs, such as operating sewing machines, which can only be done by robots at a higher cost to the company.[161] Adidas CEO Kasper Rørsted has stated that in the 120-step process of manufacturing a sneaker, "The biggest challenge the shoe industry has is how do you create a robot that puts the lace into the shoe. I'm not kidding. That's a complete manual process today. There is no technology for that."[162] Thus, low-skilled workers are still needed to perform these tasks for low wages, and high-skilled workers are needed for jobs such as machine maintenance and complex decision-making—all the while jobs requiring a moderate amount of skill are vanishing, decreasing the demand for average workers.

---

161 K. V. Ramaswamy, "Technological Change, Automation and Employment: A Short Review of Theory and Evidence," www.igidr.ac.in (Indira Gandhi Institute of Development Research, Mumbai, January 2018), http://www.igidr.ac.in/pdf/publication/WP-2018-002.pdf.

162 Marc Bain, "Hands Required: One Very Basic Job in Sneaker Manufacturing Is Testing the Limits of Automation," Quartz (Quartz, April 24, 2017), https://qz.com/966882/robots-cant-lace-shoes-so-sneaker-production-cant-be-fully-automated-just-yet/.

But doesn't this marginalization of workers in the middle contradict our earlier conclusion that machines don't kill jobs? Not exactly.

Sticking with our example of TCF manufacturing, there is no denying rapid technological advancements have been affecting the industry for decades. According to Jonathan A. Stevens, president of the American Textile History Museum, the recent expansion of automation has already had such a substantial impact on TCF that "industrial looms today incorporate air-jets to weave at speeds of 2,000 picks per minute. In 1980, 200 picks per minute was considered fast."[163] Despite the upsurge of global automation in recent years, though, worldwide employment in the industrial sector has remained remarkably consistent, hovering between 22 and 23 percent for the past twenty-six years.[164] Over the same time period, we even see that industrial employment has actually *increased* across each of the eight TCF-manufacturing Southeast Asian countries.[i][165]

---

163 John Varrasi, "Transforming the Textile Industry," ASME.org (The American Society of Mechanical Engineers, April 2012), https://www. asme.org/engineering-topics/articles/manufacturing-processing/ transforming-the-textile-industry.

164 "Employment in Industry (% of Total Employment) (Modeled ILO Estimate)," The World Bank (International Labor Organization, ILOSTAT database, 2017), https://data.worldbank.org/indicator/ SL.IND.EMPL.ZS?contextual=default&end=2017&locations=TH-KH-VN-LA-ID-PH-MM-TL-1W&start=1991&view=chart.

165 "Employment in Industry (% of Total Employment) (Modeled ILO Estimate)," World Bank (International Labor Organization,

INDUSTRIAL EMPLOYMENT AS PERCENT OF TOTAL EMPLOYMENT IN TCF-MANUFACTURING SOUTHEAST ASIAN COUNTRIES (1991 – 2017)

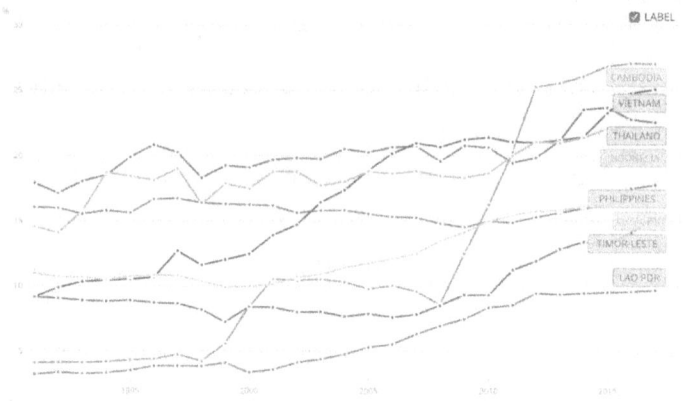

	A	B	C	D
1	Country	Percent of Workforce in Industrial Sector (1991)	Percent of Workforce in Industrial Sector (2017)	Net Change
2	Cambodia	4	27	+23
3	Indonesia	15	22	+7
4	Laos	3	10	+7
5	Myanmar	11	17	+6
6	Philippines	16	18	+2
7	Thailand	18	23	+5

ILOSTAT database, 2017), https://data.worldbank.org/indica-tor/SL.IND.EMPL.ZS?contextual=default&end=2017&loca-tions=BN-MY-SG&start=1991&type=points&view=chart.

8	Timor-Leste	9	15	+6
9	Vietnam	9	25	+16
10	SE Asia TCF Average	11	20	+9
11	World Average	23	22	-1

As Stevens made clear, rapid innovations over the past few decades have disrupted the TCF-manufacturing industry. Using his example above, in fact, automation has increased productivity by about 900 percent since 1980. But if robots were truly the job-killers we have made them out to be, you would expect the total number of jobs to decrease as they take over industries in which they can work more efficiently than humans. Yet, in all eight of the TCF-manufacturing countries in Southeast Asia, industrial employment has increased by an average of 9 percent. This proves that automation is not necessarily inimical to employment. Interestingly, all three of the Southeast Asian countries that I excluded from this dataset because they are not home to significant TCF manufacturing saw *decreases* in industrial employment over the same time period. They experienced an average net change of -9 percent, the inverse of what happened in neighboring states home to this increasingly automated industry.[166]

---

166 "Employment in Industry (% of Total Employment) (Modeled ILO Estimate)," World Bank (International Labor Organization, ILOSTAT database, 2017), https://data.worldbank.org/indicator/SL.IND.EMPL.ZS?contextual=default&end=2017&locations=BN-MY-SG&start=1991&type=points&view=chart.

	A	B	C	D
1	Country	Percent of Workforce in Industrial Sector (1991)	Percent of Workforce in Industrial Sector (2017)	Net Change
2	Brunei Darussalam	24	18	-6
3	Malaysia	28	27	-1
4	Singapore	35	16	-19
5	SE Asia non-TCF Average	29	20	-9

The problem is not that automation is killing industrial jobs, as many feared. In fact, in this instance, it seems to have even created more jobs for human workers. The nature of the ethical problem facing international companies is not that middle-skill occupations are disappearing *per se* but changing in nature. Rather, it is routine, monotonous *tasks* that are disappearing *from* these occupations because robots can be programmed to execute them. As Santos explained, "The remaining tasks and jobs require complex skills that complement technology, such as creativity, critical thinking, problem-solving, or teamwork, that is, non-routine cognitive and socio-emotional skills. Or, they require physical dexterity and human contact, features that machines lack."[167] The demand for human labor is not decreasing; new technologies simply change

---

167 Santos, "Labor Market Polarization in Developing Countries"

the kind of labor these companies demand. Understanding this distinction is crucial because it creates an opportunity for international companies like those in the TCF industry in Southeast Asia to do well by doing good.

USING CSR TO PREPARE FOR THE NEW AUTOMATED ECONOMY

The responsibility of international companies, then, is three-fold: first, through education and reskilling, they must facilitate the adaptation of the labor market to the new economic conditions created by their use of automation; second, they must reinforce the continued development of the global middle class; and third, they must automate responsibly.

EDUCATION AND RE-SKILLING

While re-skilling a large section of the workforce is no small task, some companies have already recognized their changing labor needs and started integrating it into their CSR efforts. The multinational technology conglomerate Cisco, for example, has already educated nearly a quarter of a million people on important IT concepts through its Cisco Networking Academy; partnered with the British government to launch a Computing for Schools program to offer technology teachers additional training and resources to enhance their courses; and begun to introduce courses on topics ranging from cybersecurity to the internet of things, available for free through public libraries across the United Kingdom.[168] Scot Gardner, Cisco's chief executive for the U.K. and Ireland, said these programs have "a long-term business purpose, not only because people now understand the technology and want to consume what we produce, but also because it brings a social value since the people going through those programs have more opportunities afterwards."[169] Through its socially responsible implementation of technology, Cisco is increasing demand for its products while also preparing hundreds of thousands of people to take on new roles in an increasingly automated economy.

The polarization of the labor market is not exclusive to the developed world, though, which is why it's equally important for companies to improve educational standards for stakeholders in developing countries as well. For every pair of shoes sold by the U.S. footwear business Juntos, the company donates a backpack filled with a year's worth of school supplies to a child in Ecuador.[170] While this alone is not enough to prepare Ecuadorian youth for the

---

168 Clare McDonald, "Cisco Aims to Upskill 250,000 People by 2020," ComputerWeekly.com (Computer Weekly, October 24, 2017), https://www.computerweekly.com/news/450428800/Cisco-aims-to-upskill-250000-people-by-2020.

169 Scroxton, "Automation and CSR."

170 "The Juntos Shoe: Look Good. Do Good.," juntosproject.com (Juntos Project), accessed December 29, 2018, http://www.juntosproject.com/#purposeHeaderContainer.

impending changes to the labor market, it still shows that incremental progress toward this goal can be achieved even by a relatively small company. Microsoft, on the other hand, has partnered with nonprofits around the world to improve access to computer science education and help disadvantaged youth acquire digital skills.[171] Labor polarization means that companies like Microsoft will face increased demand for workers with technological expertise in the near future, so the tech giant is investing in spreading that expertise today, benefitting both the recipients of this education and the company in the long run. Santos explained that medium-skilled jobs "are giving way either to high-skilled jobs that only a small share of workers qualify for—or to low-skilled jobs that face increasing competition."[172] In giving disadvantaged young people technical skills, Microsoft and Cisco preemptively combat the income inequality associated with labor polarization. Because of their efforts to promote the skills technology necessitates instead of those it supersedes, these companies ensure that, in the future, fewer people will have to compete for low-skilled jobs, and there will be more qualified workers to satisfy the increased demand for high-skilled labor as well.

---

171 "Global Science and Digital Skills Partnerships," Our Partners (Microsoft), accessed December 29, 2018, https://www.microsoft.com/en-us/digital-skills/partners.

172 Santos, "Labor Market Polarization in Developing Countries."

Re-skilling should also be thought of as a social responsibility that a company has to its own employees. In a 2018 survey of industrial workers by the publication *Plant Services*, respondents said the most effective way their employers could recruit and retain employees would be offering better training and career development opportunities, which they ranked as even more important than higher wages and better benefits.[173] But an increased ability to attract and keep the talent they need isn't all that companies have to gain from re-skilling. Summarizing their research on the future of human capital, a team from Deloitte offered business leaders the following advice:

> *Our research clearly shows that one of the new rules for the digital age is to expand our vision of the workforce; think about jobs in the context of tasks that can be automated (or outsourced) and the new role of human skills; and focus even more heavily on the customer experience, employee experience, and employment value proposition for people. Organizations that automate manufacturing plants, for example, and that do not clearly give people opportunities for reskilling and new positions, may see their brand suffer, and to some extent may also feel pressure from the social and political environment. AT&T's talent manifesto, which*

---

173 LaFave, "Help (Still) Wanted."

encourages and empowers employees to continuously
reskill themselves, is an effective example of a com-
pany that automates in an integrated, human-centric
way.[174]

In the words of Scott Smith, AT&T's senior vice president of human resources operations, "You can go out to the street and hire for the skills, but we all know that the supply of technical talent is limited, and everybody is going after it. Or you can do your best to step up and reskill your existing workforce to fill the gap."[175] The latter option is better not only for the company but for its employees as well.

Companies that do not make an effort to help their workers develop a malleable skillset risk tarnishing the image of their brand. Those that do, on the other hand, boost morale and reap the benefits of having more ambitious, motivated, and adaptable employees.

Companies that offer educational benefits to employees' families experience similar benefits. Professor Michael Ryan of Georgetown University's McDonough School of Business

---

174 Jeff Schwartz et al., "The Future of Work: The Augmented Workforce," 2017 Global Human Capital Trends (Deloitte Insights, February 28, 2017), https://www2.deloitte.com/insights/us/en/focus/human-capital-trends/2017/future-workforce-changing-nature-of-work.html.

175 John Donovan and Cathy Benko, "Inside AT&T's Radical Talent Overhaul," Harvard Business Review (Harvard University, October 7, 2016), https://hbr.org/2016/10/atts-talent-overhaul.

recalled speaking with a bank that "created an educational program for the children of their employees who didn't have access to good schools, and that was quite popular. ... They didn't do it because they thought it would be a smart business move for them. But employment retention went up, so CSR and a smart business model have some complementary aspects."

Despite the risks associated with emerging technologies, their application in international businesses can itself serve as a form of CSR. When a foreign company begins operating in a developing country, it brings with it a constantly evolving set of technologies that would not otherwise be available there. In some cases, simply by entering a country with many poor people, a company is "not just putting them to work but arming them with managerial know-how," Ryan added. "Unless they're a Chinese company, they're not going to put in 5,000 of their own workers. They're going to put in just a few senior managers because it's quite expensive. Those few people then encourage the local people that they hire, whether management or labor, to learn, which transfers the company's knowledge to them. They're basically doing CSR just by transfer of technology and knowledge." The needs of the business then coincide with its social responsibility to its employees in the host country, as both parties benefit from the company training its workers to apply these new technologies.

International companies that transfer technical know-how to workers in their host countries can also increase social mobility in regions where it has historically been nearly impossible to achieve, benefitting the local communities tremendously. Higher levels of proficiency in advanced technology beget higher wages and, in turn, economic empowerment, so the host community becomes richer as well. This is also good for the company, which has then enabled many people with newfound wealth to become consumers of its goods.

INVESTING IN DEVELOPMENT

Another reason international businesses should be concerned about labor polarization is that it threatens to create increased competition for low-skill jobs. Although there will be an increase in demand for labor at both extremes of the skill spectrum, countless people possessing only an average skillset will not qualify for the new jobs at the top of the spectrum, so they will be forced to compete with a sizable body of unskilled workers for the jobs at the bottom. This increased competition will likely result in even lower wages for already low-paying jobs and higher unemployment for those who cannot find such jobs.

The proliferation of poverty imposes a substantial burden on the corporation, not only because the poor cannot become its customers, but also because the state incurs additional costs (loss of tax revenue, plus increased reliance on state services such as unemployment pay and health care), which will then need to be passed onto the corporation through higher taxes. It is therefore in every company's best long-term interest to act now to decrease future pressure on the labor market (and to combat poverty in general) by training more workers for high-skilled jobs.

Furthermore, the extreme poverty resulting from labor polarization can bring economic and political development under threat, which is also detrimental to business. Most scholars generally accept that higher levels of economic development facilitate the transition to democracy.[176] The growth of democracy is advantageous for international companies in two ways: because it helps them fulfill their social responsibility to the community by contributing to greater political freedom, and because democratic institutions such as stability, transparency, and the rule of law help establish favorable conditions for conducting business by eliminating potential barriers to free trade and investment, reducing red tape, and guaranteeing the enforcement of contracts.[177] Businesses therefore have a potent long-term interest in fostering

176 Ronald Inglehart and Christian Welzel, "How Development Leads to Democracy: What We Know About Modernization," Foreign Affairs (Foreign Affairs Magazine, 2009), https://www.foreignaffairs.com/articles/2009-03-01/how-development-leads-democracy.

177 "Democracy Is Good for Business," Freedom at Issue Blog (Freedom House, August 3, 2015), https://freedomhouse.org/blog/democracy-good-business.

democracy, a goal achievable through CSR efforts focused on promoting education, advocacy, and economic and political development—all of which can be facilitated by the use of technology.

As I noted earlier, corporations should not play a direct role in democracy-building. They should, however, give their host countries the tools necessary for development in the hopes that they democratize independently. By contributing to the creation of conditions conducive to democracy, a company can benefit itself and the world.

SOCIALLY RESPONSIBLE AUTOMATION

Responsible implementation of technology is also achievable within the company. Companies may invest in robots for applications besides increased productivity, such as improved health and safety for employees. "Robots can help prevent injuries or adverse health effects resulting from working in hazardous conditions," asserted Vladimir Murashov, a senior scientist in the Office of the Director at the U.S. National Institute for Occupational Safety and Health and a member of the office's Center for Occupational Robotics Research. "Some examples are musculoskeletal disorders due to repetitive or awkward motions, or traumatic injuries (for example, in poultry processing, where cuts are common). They can also prevent multiple hazards in emergency response situations such as chemical spills."[178] This feature is obviously good for employees, who can work in a safer environment, but it also benefits the company by reducing liability in addition to improving efficiency.

These robots do not have to remove middle-skilled workers from the equation, either. Companies have the socially responsible option of focusing their technological acquisitions on human-robot collaboration (HRC), whereby a robot assists a human operator. "This means the machine does not replace the human, but complements his capabilities and relieves him of arduous tasks," explained Kuka AG, a German manufacturer of industrial robotics. "They optimally support you as an assistant in the case of workload peaks and resource bottlenecks in your production operations. ... Take BMW in Dingolfing, for example. Where in the past workers had to lift and join heavy bevel gears for front-axle gear units unaided, they now work together with their sensitive robot colleague, the LBR iiwa, hand in hand in confined spaces – entirely without safety fencing and in their customary surroundings."[179]

---

178 Susan Vargas, "Robots in the Workplace," Safety Health Magazine (National Safety Council Congress and Expo, March 25, 2018), https://www.safetyandhealthmagazine.com/articles/16789-robots-in-the-workplace.

179 "Human-Robot Collaboration (HRC)," kuka.com (KUKA), accessed December 28, 2018, https://www.kuka.com/nb-no/technologies/human-robot-collaboration.

Perhaps the greatest appeal of HRC is that it does not contribute to labor polarization. Instead of robots executing tasks that would otherwise belong to humans, humans use robots to execute those tasks. Companies can use HRC to automate responsibly, maximizing productivity by making middle-skilled jobs safer and less strenuous. The resulting increased efficiency generates more profit for the company, which can be reinvested to create better products for consumers and increase, rather than reduce the compensation and number of workers. This effect is especially beneficial in developing countries where labor is cheap and companies often abuse their workers—automation can empower companies to pay living wages to more people, lifting them out of poverty while also keeping them in safer, better working conditions.

In the coming years, transformations in international business and technology threaten to upend the global labor market and create an array of problems in developing and developed countries alike. Many of these transformations are already underway, and while automation itself is not killing jobs *per se*, it does pose risks for the future of the global economy. International corporations have the power, the responsibility, and a compelling long-term interest to address these issues now. For their own sake and for the sake of workers everywhere, these companies must take steps toward re-skilling the workforce, encouraging global development, and automating responsibly.

[i] For the purposes of this discussion, I define "TCF-manufacturing Southeast Asian countries" with the following methodology. I begin with the United Nations Statistics Division's definition of "South-eastern Asia" as the following 11 countries: Brunei Darussalam, Cambodia, Indonesia, Laos, Malaysia, Myanmar, Philippines, Singapore, Thailand, Timor-Leste, and Vietnam. I then remove those countries whose CIA World Factbook entries do not list the any of the following as major industries: textiles, garments, woven cloth, clothes, footwear, or shoes. This eliminates Singapore, Malaysia, and Brunei Darussalam, leaving a final dataset of eight countries.

CHAPTER 8

THE SOCIALLY CONSCIOUS CONSUMER

———

Every time you spend money, you're casting a vote for the kind of world you want.

—ANNA LAPPE[180]

I realize there may be no place for emotions in a book about business, but please indulge me for a moment as I write about them anyway.

Nearly all that I have written here has focused on the role of international corporations themselves, but I would now like

180 Anna Lappe, "Lifestyle," blueocean.net (Blue Ocean Network), accessed February 24, 2019, https://blueocean.net/lifestyle/page/10/.

to turn my attention elsewhere, to you. You, the reader, the human being with your own life and your own individual identity.

While reading about the various successes, failures, and future prospects of international corporate social responsibility, you've likely felt a range of different emotions. Perhaps you've felt sad about the state of our world, or perhaps you've felt angry that not enough progress has been made to improve it. Perhaps you've felt hopeful, as I do, that in the future those in power will do the right thing, not only for themselves, but for all of us.

Most of us, however, do not work in boardrooms. Most of us do not even work in offices, in fact. We don't have the ability to directly decide whether to save millions of dollars in production costs by outsourcing to a factory so cruel that it had to set up literal nets to prevent workers from leaping to their deaths en masse.[181] Nor do we get to directly decide whether a company can list "improving the lives of children" as a core priority[182] even though it sells predominantly

---

181 Jamie Fullerton, "Suicide at Chinese IPhone Factory Reignites Concern over Working Conditions," The Telegraph (Telegraph Media Group, January 7, 2018), https://www.telegraph.co.uk/news/2018/01/07/suicide-chinese-iphone-factory-reignites-concern-working-conditions/.

182 "2014 McDonald's Sustainability Report," The Good Business Report (McDonald's, 2014), https://corporate.mcdonalds.com/content/dam/gwscorp/scale-for-good/2014_sustainability_report.pdf.

unhealthy food,[183] its mascot is a clown, and it is increasingly advertising to children as young as two.[184] And perhaps that has left you feeling powerless.

But you shouldn't feel that way. Although the global scope of these problems may make them appear distant and any efforts to resolve them seem futile, that's not the case. Unless you live in the wilderness as a hunter-gatherer, you occupy a very important position amid all this chaos. You are a consumer of not just one of these corporations, but of so many that an attempt to list them could be a book of its own. For every item you purchase, every service you receive, you are interacting with one of these entities, and they need you more than you need them. If one company lets you down in some way, you are free to purchase the same goods or services from any of its competitors instead. Part of the beauty of the free market is that it empowers consumers to make choices with their money, and any company that fails to satisfy its consumers will not be a company for very long. Therein lies the importance of the consumer in CSR.

---

183 Brad Tuttle, "McDonald's Sales Rise with Focus on Core Menu, Not Health | Money," Everyday Money (Meredith Corporation, April 22, 2016), http://time.com/money/4303546/mcdonalds-big-mac-fries-health/.

184 Jennifer L. Harris, Marlene B. Scwartz, and Kelly D. Brownell, "Fast Food Advertising to Children and Teens Score," fastfoodmarketing. org (Yale Rudd Center for Food Policy and Obesity, 2010), http://fastfoodmarketing.org/media/FastFoodFACTS_Report_Summary_2010.pdf.

In a sense, the very term "corporate social responsibility" is misleading, as it implies that the obligation to better society falls on the corporation alone. I would contend that we as individuals must also shoulder some of this obligation. The corporation cannot exist, let alone bring about any social good, without the consent and cooperation of the consumer. We each have a responsibility to use the market as a tool for progress.

A growing body of literature suggests that consumers have an undeniable, substantial effect on CSR outcomes. "Consumers have been shown to reward companies that engage in CSR with interest, loyalty and trust," a 2016 paper on the topic pointed out. "However, skepticism of companies that engage in CSR still remains and tends to hinder the success of CSR campaigns. Although close to half (46%) of consumers have a highly positive attitude toward socially responsible companies, one-third of individuals view CSR initiatives as self-interested behavior by corporations.[185] This explains why a segment of consumers has a negative attitude toward firms that are involved in CSR."[186] Just as consumers select winners

---

185 Sarah Alhouti, Catherine M. Johnson, and Betsey Bugg Holloway, "Corporate Social Responsibility Authenticity: Investigating Its Antecedents and Outcomes," Journal of Business Research (Elsevier, March 2016), https://www.sciencedirect.com/science/article/pii/S0148296315004063.

186 Ibid.

and losers in the market, they also play a role in determining which CSR campaigns succeed and which do not.

While some may argue that institutions should be responsible for CSR oversight, they often lack the influence of consumers. Nonprofits, NGOs, international institutions, and members of civil society have made several attempts to standardize CSR, but these have had little effect. Despite these groups' introduction of various sets of global CSR rules such as the OECD Guidelines for Multinational Enterprises and the ISO 26000, many international businesses have persisted in committing large-scale misdeeds, as corporations are ultimately unaccountable to these groups.

Governments have had slightly more success in this regard, yet they too still largely lack sufficient leverage over international conglomerates.[187] The consulting firm Accenture, for example, does tens of billions of dollars of business across more than 120 countries, enabling it to work around many of the demands of individual governments.[188] We don't just

---

187 Parag Khanna and David Francis, "These 25 Companies Are More Powerful Than Many Countries," Foreign Policy (Foreign Policy, 2016), https://foreignpolicy.com/2016/03/15/these-25-companies-are-more-powerful-than-many-countries-multinational-corporate-wealth-power/.

188 "Accenture Reports Very Strong Fourth-Quarter and Full-Year Fiscal 2015 Results," newsroom.accenture.com (Accenture, September 24, 2015), https://newsroom.accenture.com/news/accenture-reports-very-strong-fourth-quarter-and-full-year-fiscal-2015-results.htm.

live in an era of multinationals, but one of "metanationals: companies that, like Accenture, are effectively stateless," international relations expert Parag Khanna reflected in an article for *Foreign Policy*. Such companies whose operations transcend borders "choose locations for personnel, factories, executive suites, or bank accounts based on where regulations are friendly, resources abundant, and connectivity seamless. Clever metanationals often have legal domicile in one country, corporate management in another, financial assets in a third, and administrative staff spread over several more."[189] The task of holding metanational companies responsible for the societal effects of their business cannot be left exclusively to governments, as these companies can sidestep the efforts of individual states by simply moving their assets around the globe as needed to find the regulatory conditions most advantageous to them.

Consumers have, by contrast, the most power in determining CSR outcomes, because corporations are ultimately accountable to them like no other. Companies carefully calculate their every action with one goal in mind: getting consumers to give them their money. When consumers engage in a transaction with a company, they express approval for that that company's behavior and enable this behavior to continue. When people disapprove of a company's conduct, no matter

---

189 Khanna and Francis, "Companies More Powerful Than Many Countries."

the size of the company or the vastness of its assets, they can freely decide to terminate their business with it at any time, cutting off its lifeblood.

If consumers demand that companies operate responsibly, they can force them to do so by practicing socially responsible consumer behavior (SRCB). And yet, for the most part, they don't. In a study on the relationship between CSR and buying behavior, researchers concluded that although "most of the respondents are positive toward business in general and toward socially responsible companies ... most respondents do not regularly use CSR as a purchasing criterion."[190] Consumers say they approve of CSR, but when it comes to actually wielding their power to enforce CSR standards, they fall short.

The same study explained part of the cause for this inconsistency between hypothetical approval for CSR and the lack of action to support it: "Two major factors emerge as reasons for the lack of SRCB: (1) self-interest manifested in buying based on the traditional criteria of price, quality, and convenience, combined with the assumption

---

190 Lois A. Mohr, Deborah J. Webb, and Katherine E. Harris, "Do Consumers Expect Companies to Be Socially Responsible? The Impact of Corporate Social Responsibility on Buying Behavior," JSTOR (The Journal of Consumer Affairs, 2001), https://www-jstor-org.proxy.library.georgetown.edu/stable/23860071?seq=23#metadata_info_tab_contents.

that using CSR would compromise their choices on these criteria, and (2) low level of knowledge and difficulty obtaining information on the social responsibility records of companies."[191] The first factor, in other words, is rooted in the presumption that CSR necessitates some kind of sacrifice on the part of the consumer, whether it be increased costs, worse products, or some otherwise avoidable burden. The second factor preventing consumers from making socially responsible purchases is that most people simply do not know enough about different brands' CSR records to make informed decisions based on them. The average consumer shows a casual commitment to CSR, but these two points induce hesitation to make SRCB anything more than a passive behavior, leading to general inaction.

As I have already suggested in earlier chapters of this book, self-interest, the first category of factors causing people not to practice SRCB, does not constitute a compelling reason to avoid socially responsible companies. This is because no inherent aspect of CSR necessitates a compromise on price, quality, or convenience for the customer. Often, CSR is even quite conducive to improving these criteria for customers. When a company starts using less environmentally taxing methods to manufacture its products, for example, its

---

191 Ibid.

decreased energy costs generate savings that are then passed onto the consumer. It is therefore often within a person's own best interest to actively seek out socially responsible companies to patronize.

The second category—lack of access to information on companies' CSR records—may at first seem reasonable but ultimately also does not represent a valid reason to abstain from SRCB. As CSR becomes increasingly ubiquitous, especially among international enterprises, more and more businesses have begun to publish annual CSR reports. Thanks to recent advancements in technology, these reports are almost always publicly available online and can be found with a quick internet search. While these reports are typically written and published by the companies themselves and therefore tend to be misleading in some cases, they do provide a general idea of where a company's priorities lie. Reports by third-party nonprofits and news articles detailing major companies' CSR dealings from a neutral perspective are also widely available online to help consumers verify the information these companies put out. I strongly encourage you to read the CSR reports of companies you frequently patronize. You may be pleasantly surprised or disappointed by their conduct, and you will likely want to adjust your spending habits accordingly.

So what can you do with this information? How can you practically exercise your ethical influence over international corporations?

Because all this occurs on such a large scale, you as an individual consumer cannot take unilateral action to bring about any CSR outcome. Recall, however, that all market outcomes represent the results of aggregate decision-making—millions of consumers each pursuing what they want—and that this demand drives changes in everything from wages to stock prices. Your corporate social responsibility, as a consumer, is to shape your behavior according to what you believe is right for the world. But, of course, one person's change in purchasing decisions causes virtually zero change the market, especially change of an international scope.

For consumers to bring about meaningful changes in international CSR, they must overcome the challenge of coordinating their efforts among millions of people across borders and oceans. Just as companies rely on highly developed technologies to function efficiently and effectively, consumers can leverage technology to collectively influence corporations from the outside.

The same principle applies to consumers attempting to influence these corporations from the outside. They need to actively seek out CSR information relevant to causes that matter most to them and transmit this information to others in their network, both of which can now be achieved more easily than ever through new telecommunication capabilities, as well as through social media. Perhaps this is why millennials practice SRCB more than any previous generation—so much so that many companies are even reinventing their marketing strategies to focus more on social responsibility—suggesting that perhaps in the coming years consumers will play a more active role in holding international corporations to their CSR commitments.[192]

In a speech before the House of Commons on November 11, 1947, Winston Churchill famously stated, "No one pretends that democracy is perfect or all-wise. Indeed, it has been said that democracy is the worst form of government except all those other forms that have been tried from time to time."[193] I believe that the same could be said of capitalism. Yes, capitalism as a system largely driven by greed that, as we have seen, results in unethical behavior at times, but it is still by far the best system available to us, so we can't

192 Sarah Landrum, "Millennials Driving Brands To Practice Socially Responsible Marketing," Forbes (Forbes Magazine, March 17, 2017), https://www.forbes.com/sites/sarahlandrum/2017/03/17/millennials-driving-brands-to-practice-socially-responsible-marketing/#56eb1a0d4990.

193 Winston Churchill, "The Worst Form of Government," The International Churchill Society (The International Churchill Society, March 20, 2017), https://winstonchurchill.org/resources/quotes/the-worst-form-of-government/.

give up on it because of its imperfections. Rather, we must embrace its enormous capacity to serve as an engine of global human progress. It's up to all stakeholders, from CEOs to consumers, to work together to turn capitalism into a force for global good.

ACKNOWLEDGEMENTS

—

First of all, I owe an astronomical debt to my family, without whom none of this would have been possible: Mom, Dad, Jared, Grammy, Grampy, Harriet, Grandma, Papa, Matt, Misako, Deb, Mark, Norm, Bryan, Lindsey, Troy, Eric, Ray, Jaden, Noah, and, of course, my Superfans, Bill and Steph.

I thank my extraordinary, brilliant, and endlessly supportive girlfriend Alex Toutounji, who has encouraged me and kept me going through even the most difficult parts of this journey.

I also owe thanks to my earliest supporters, including J.J. Woronoff, Alex Pfirrmann, Connor Harding, Ted Root, Kelly McCarthy, Andrew Feinstein, Dylan McCarthy, Chris O'Keefe, Adam Treger, Bernie Rosenthal, Leonardo Mendez, Daniel Silbert, Ron Talmor, Ethan McGregor, Steve Antico,

Ben Barrett, Sandro Oretga-Riek, Leo Psaros, Matt Hand-macher, Josh Levitt, Nick Sherr, Michael Tuchler, Kathy Scholtz, Karen Iworsky, Greg Jardis, the McCowans, the Trezises, Drew Jansson, Christian Sturzo, Allie Rutledge, Hayley Tagliente, Gabe Cohn, and many others whose names could fill an entire book of their own.

Lastly, I acknowledge the hard work of Eric Koester, New Degree Press, and all my passionate interviewers for helping me make this dream a reality.

APPENDIX

—

INTRODUCTION

"2014 Assessments Of Shared Hazelnut Supply Chain In Turkey: Nestlé, Balsu, And Olam | Fair Labor Association". 2015. *Fairlabor.Org.* http://www.fairlabor.org/2014-hazelnuts-independent-external-assessments.

Clark, Kylienne, Travis Shaul, Brian H. Lower, and Amanda L. Varcho. 2015. "2.2 A Bitter Brew- Coffee Production, Deforestation, Soil Erosion And Water Contamination". *Ohiostate.Pressbooks.Pub.* https://ohiostate.pressbooks.pub/sciencebites/chapter/a-bitter-brew-coffee-production-deforestation-soil-erosion-and-water-contamination/.

"Future Demand And Climate Change Could Make Coffee A Driver Of Deforestation - Conservation International". 2016. *Conservation International.* https://www.conservation.org/NewsRoom/pressreleases/Pages/Future-Demand-and-Climate-Change-Could-Make-Coffee-a-Driver-of-Deforestation-.aspx.

Goldschein, Eric. 2011. "11 Incredible Facts About The Global Coffee Industry". *Business Insider.* https://www.businessinsider.com/facts-about-the-coffee-industry-2011-11.

Griffin, Paul. 2017. "CDP Carbon Majors Report 2017". *The Carbon Majors Database.* https://b8f65cb373b1b7b-15feb-c70d8ead6ced550b4d987d7c03fcdd1d.ssl.cf3.rackcdn.com/cms/reports/documents/000/002/327/original/Carbon-Majors-Report-2017.pdf?1499691240.

Higonnet, Etelle, Marisa Bellantonio, and Glenn Hurowitz. 2017. "Chocolate's Dark Secret: How The Cocoa Industry Destroys National Parks". *Mightyearth.Org.* http://www.mightyearth.org/wp-content/uploads/2017/09/chocolates_dark_secret_english_web.pdf.

Jimenez, Guillermo, and Elizabeth Pulos. 2014. "Corruption In International Business". *Good Corporation, Bad Corporation: Corporate Social Responsibility In The Global Economy.* https://milnepublishing.geneseo.edu/good-cor-

poration-bad-corporation/chapter/10-corruption-in-in-
ternational-business/.

Lai, Anjali. 2018. "Millennials Call For Values-Driven Companies, But They're Not The Only Ones Interested". *Forbes.
Com*. https://www.forbes.com/sites/forrester/2018/05/23/
millennials-call-for-values-driven-companies-but-they-
re-not-the-only-ones-interested/#436542555464.

Mishel, Lawrence, and Jessica Schieder. 2017. "CEO Pay
Remains High Relative To The Pay Of Typical Workers
And High-Wage Earners". *Epi.Org*. https://www.epi.org/
publication/ceo-pay-remains-high-relative-to-the-pay-
of-typical-workers-and-high-wage-earners/.

Newport, Frank. 2018. "Democrats More Positive About
Socialism Than Capitalism". *Gallup.com*. https://news.
gallup.com/poll/240725/democrats-positive-social-
ism-capitalism.aspx.

Patrick, Kate. 2018. "Corporate Responsibility Starts With
The Supply Chain". *Supply Chain Dive*. https://www.sup-
plychaindive.com/news/corporate-responsibility-sup-
ply-chain/521141/.

Ponte, Stefano. 2002. "The 'Latte Revolution'? Regulation,
Markets And Consumption In The Global Coffee Chain".

Semanticscholar.Org. https://www.semanticscholar. org/paper/The-'Latte-Revolution'-Regulation,-Mar- kets-and-in-Ponte/7b2f9274b27c0babc6148434bdb- d8a2b62a7b5da.

"Responsibly Grown Coffee". 2010. *Starbucks Coffee Company.* https://www.starbucks.ie/responsibility/sourcing/coffee

Shen, Lucinda. 2017. "Corporate Misdeeds: 10 Biggest Cor- porate Scandals Of 2017". *Finance: Corporate Scandals.* http://fortune.com/2017/12/31/biggest-corporate-scan- dals-misconduct-2017-pr/.

Shen, Lucinda. 2017. "Are Facebook, Google, Twitter Manipulating Users? Washington Wants To Know". *Www.Fortune.Com.* http://fortune.com/2017/12/27/face- book-google-twitter-addiction/.

"Sweetbridge". 2019. *Sweetbridge.Com.* https://sweetbridge. com/platform/.

Weinberg, Bennett Alan. 2001. "The World Of Caffeine: The Science And Culture Of The World's Most Popu- lar Drug". Google Books. https://books.google.com/ books?id=Qyz5CnOaH9oC&pg=PA3&dq=coffee+- goat+ethiopia+Kaldi&lr=&ei=paxHStuDJ4XuzATj97h- f#v=onepage&q=coffee goat ethiopia Kaldi&f=false.

CHAPTER 1

"2014 Assessments Of Shared Hazelnut Supply Chain In Turkey: Nestlé, Balsu, And Olam | Fair Labor Association". 2015. *Fairlabor.Org.* http://www.fairlabor.org/2014-hazelnuts-independent-external-assessments.

Griffin, Paul. 2017. "CDP Carbon Majors Report 2017". *The Carbon Majors Database.* https://b8f65cb373b1b7b-15feb-c70d8ead6ced550b4d987d7c03fcdd1d.ssl.cf3.rack-cdn.com/cms/reports/documents/000/002/327/original/Carbon-Majors-Report-2017.pdf?1499691240.

Higonnet, Etelle, Marisa Bellantonio, and Glenn Hurowitz. 2017. "Chocolate's Dark Secret: How The Cocoa Industry Destroys National Parks". *Mightyearth.Org.* http://www.mightyearth.org/wp-content/uploads/2017/09/chocolates_dark_secret_english_web.pdf.

Jimenez, Guillermo, and Elizabeth Pulos. 2014. "Corruption In International Business". *Good Corporation, Bad Corporation: Corporate Social Responsibility In The Global Economy.* https://milnepublishing.geneseo.edu/good-corporation-bad-corporation/chapter/10-corruption-in-international-business/.

Newport, Frank. 2018. "Democrats More Positive About Socialism Than Capitalism". *Gallup.com.* https://news.

gallup.com/poll/240725/democrats-positive-social-ism-capitalism.aspx.

Shaban, Hamza. 2017. "Equifax CEO Richard Smith Steps Down Amid Hacking Scandal". *Washingtonpost.Com.* https://www.washingtonpost.com/news/the-switch/wp/2017/09/26/equifax-ceo-retires-following-massive-data-breach/?utm_term=.faa2ac64da40.

Shen, Lucinda. 2017. "Corporate Misdeeds: 10 Biggest Corporate Scandals Of 2017". *Finance: Corporate Scandals.* http://fortune.com/2017/12/31/biggest-corporate-scandals-misconduct-2017-pr/.

Shen, Lucinda. 2017. "Are Facebook, Google, Twitter Manipulating Users? Washington Wants To Know". *Www.Fortune.Com.* http://fortune.com/2017/12/27/facebook-google-twitter-addiction/.

Smith, Tim. "Verbatim: How Businesses View Sustainability & CSR Reporting." Business Ethics. November 14, 2017. Accessed June 15, 2019. http://business-ethics.com/2010/07/27/4298-in-their-own-words-how-businesses-view-sustainability-and-csr-reporting/.

CHAPTER 2

Caldwell, Christopher. "Sending Jobs Overseas." *The Claremont Institute*. Winter 2017, accessed May 11, 2018, http://www.claremont.org/crb/article/sending-jobs-overseas/.

Fry, Erika. "Can Levi's Make Life Better for Garment Workers?" Fortune, September 8, 2017. http://fortune.com/2017/09/08/levis-change-the-world.

Kitroeff, Natalie. "Unemployment Rate Hits 3.9%, a Rare Low, as Job Market Becomes More Competitive." *The New York Times*. May 04, 2018, accessed May 11, 2018, https://www.nytimes.com/2018/05/04/business/economy/jobs-report.html.

Kuttner, Robert. "White Nationalism and Economic Nationalism." *The American Prospect*, October 10, 2017, accessed May 11, 2018, http://prospect.org/article/white-nationalism-and-economic-nationalism.

Lambert, Renaud. "Does the FN Have an Economic Strategy?" *Le Monde Diplomatique*, May 01, 2017, accessed May 11, 2018, https://mondediplo.com/2017/05/07FN.

Lind, Michael, "The New Class War." *American Affairs Journal*. August 06, 2017, accessed May 11, 2018, https://americanaffairsjournal.org/2017/05/new-class-war/.

Mourdoukoutas, Panos. "Globalization Has Done a Lot of Great Things for Americans." *Forbes.* January 04, 2017, accessed May 11, 2018, https://www.forbes.com/sites/panosmourdoukoutas/2017/01/03/globalization-has-done-many-great-things-for-americans/#57df2e93583d.

"Political Corporate Social Responsibility and Development," Ismail Adelopo, Kemi Yekini, and Lukman Raimi, http://eprints.uwe.ac.uk/26635/1/Political%20Corporate%20Social%20Responsibility%20and%20Development.docx

Rushe, Dominic. "US Economy Adds Jobs for Record 100th Consecutive Month." The Guardian. Guardian News and Media, February 1, 2019. https://www.theguardian.com/business/2019/feb/01/us-jobs-report-news-latest-record-breaking-month-100th-in-a-row.

Scherer, Andreas-Georg, and Guido Palazzo. "The New Political Role of Business in a Globalized World: A Review of a New Perspective on CSR and Its Implications for the Firm, Governance, and Democracy." Journal of Management Studies. John Wiley & Sons, Ltd (10.1111), April 27, 2011. https://onlinelibrary.wiley.com/doi/full/10.1111/j.1467-6486.2010.00950.x.

Smith, Stacey Vanek. "How Much Would an All-American IPhone Cost?" Marketplace, May 20, 2014. https://www.

marketplace.org/2014/05/20/business/ive-always-won-dered/how-much-would-all-american-iphone-cost.

"Source." Levi Strauss & Co. Accessed 2018. https://www.levistrauss.com/suppliers-operations/.

Tarpey, Matthew. "3 Things to Know about the April 2019 Jobs Report." CareerBuilder, 2019. https://www.career-builder.com/advice/bls-jobs-report.

Varinsky, Dana. "Here's What 5 of Your Favorite Products Would Cost If They Were Made in the US." Business Insider. Business Insider, November 27, 2016. https://www.businessinsider.com/how-much-products-would-cost-if-made-in-us-2016-11#jeans-2.

CHAPTER 3

Blanche, Caitlin C., Elizabeth Abbott Gilman, William D. Semins, Daniel J. Stephenson, and Amy L. Groff. "Global Supply Chain Risk: Corporate Exposure for Human Trafficking, Forced Labor and Human Rights Abuses | Stay Informed | K&L Gates." K&L Gates LLP, October 24, 2017. http://www.klgates.com/global-supply-chain-risk-corpo-rate-exposure-for-human-trafficking-forced-labor-and-human-rights-abuses-10-24-2017/.

Broadman, Harry G. "When Too Much Corporate Social
Responsibility (CSR) Is Too Good To Be True." Forbes.
Forbes Magazine, September 3, 2018. https://www.forbes.
com/sites/harrybroadman/2018/05/30/when-too-much-
corporate-social-responsibility-is-too-good-to-be-
true/#290503be499f.

Fernholz, Tim. "The Absence of a Mysterious Research
Center in Angola Could Be Evidence of Oil Corruption."
Quartz. Quartz, August 12, 2014. https://qz.com/247521/
the-absence-of-a-mysterious-research-center-in-angola-
could-be-evidence-of-oil-corruption/.

Gillison, Samantha. "'Clean Eating' Is Such a Sham That
Fast Food Chains Push It." NBC Opinion. NBCUniversal News Group, February 6, 2018. https://www.nbcnews.
com/think/opinion/clean-eating-has-become-such-sh-
am-fast-food-chains-are-ncna845081.

Meier, Stephan, and Lea Cassar. "Stop Talking About
How CSR Helps Your Bottom Line." Harvard Business
Review. Harvard University, January 31, 2018. https://hbr.
org/2018/01/stop-talking-about-how-csr-helps-your-bot-
tom-line.

Price, Andrew. "Why Companies Make False Corporate
Social Responsibility Promises." Fast Company. Fast

Company, February 21, 2012. https://www.fastcompany.
com/1679334/why-companies-make-false-corporate-so-
cial-responsibility-promises.

"Taking Stock of India's Mandatory CSR Legislation Four
Years Out." Taking Stock of India's Mandartory CSR Legislation Four Years Out. The Kenan Institute for Ethics
at Duke University, August 23, 2018. https://kenan.ethics.
duke.edu/csr-workshop/.

"Tobacco Industry and Corporate Responsibility: an Inherent
Contradiction." Tobacco Free Initiative. World Health
Organization, 2004. http://www.who.int/tobacco/com-
munications/CSR_report.pdf.

Winegarden, Wayne. "Unilever And The Failure Of Corporate Social Responsibility." Econostats. Forbes Magazine,
March 15, 2017. https://www.forbes.com/sites/econos-
tats/2017/03/15/unilever-and-the-failure-of-corporate-so-
cial-responsibility/#670eafc498d2.

CHAPTER 4

"Air Pollution Deaths Cost Global Economy US$225 Billion."
World Bank. World Bank Group, September 8, 2016. http://
www.worldbank.org/en/news/press-release/2016/09/08/
air-pollution-deaths-cost-global-economy-225-billion.

Bai, Jie, Edmund Malesky, and Benjamin Olken. "Growing out of Corruption." Center for Economic Policy Research: Policy Portal. VOX, November 22, 2013. https://voxeu.org/article/growing-out-corruption.

Berger-Walliser, Gerlinde, and Inara Scott. "Redefining Corporate Social Responsibility in an Era of Globalization and Regulatory Hardening." American Business Law Journal. John Wiley & Sons, Ltd (10.1111), February 2, 2018. https://onlinelibrary.wiley.com/doi/full/10.1111/ablj.12119.

Britannica, The Editors of Encyclopaedia. "Free-Trade Zone." Encyclopædia Britannica. Encyclopædia Britannica, inc., February 26, 2016. https://www.britannica.com/topic/free-trade-zone.

"Combatting Corruption." ICC. International Chamber of Commerce. Accessed December 23, 2018. https://iccwbo.org/global-issues-trends/responsible-business/combatting-corruption/.

"CONVENTION ON COMBATING BRIBERY OF FOREIGN PUBLIC OFFICIALS IN INTERNATIONAL BUSINESS TRANSACTIONS." OECD. The Organisation for Economic Co-operation and Development, 2011. http://www.oecd.org/daf/anti-bribery/ConvCombatBribery_ENG.pdf.

Hills, Greg, Leigh Fiske, and Adeeb Z. Mahmud. "Anti-Corruption as Strategic CSR: A Call to Action for Corporations." FSG. FSG Social Impact Advisors, Merck Company Foundation, and the Ethics Resource Center, May 2009. https://www.fsg.org/publications/anti-corruption-strategic-csr#download-area.

"Investing in Coffee Communities." Starbucks Coffee Company. Starbucks Coffee Company. Accessed December 28, 2018. https://www.starbucks.com/responsibility/community/farmer-support/social-development-investments.

Jimenez, Guillermo, and Elizabeth Pulos. 2014. "Corruption In International Business". *Good Corporation, Bad Corporation: Corporate Social Responsibility In The Global Economy.* https://milnepublishing.geneseo.edu/good-corporation-bad-corporation/chapter/10-corruption-in-international-business/.

Kottasová, Ivana. "These Companies Are Leading the Fight against Climate Change." CNN. Cable News Network, October 9, 2018. https://www.cnn.com/2018/10/09/business/climate-change-companies/index.html.

"Mexico Corruption Report." Business Anti-Corruption Portal. GAN Integrity, Inc., 2018. https://www.business-anti-corruption.com/country-profiles/mexico/.

"Natural Catastrophes and Climate Change." Swiss Re 2017 Corporate Responsibility Report. Swiss Re, 2017. http://reports.swissre.com/corporate-responsibility-report/2017/cr-report/solutions/natural-catastrophes-and-climate-change.html.

Peretz, Marissa. "These Companies Prove You Can Be Socially Conscious And Profitable." Forbes. Forbes Magazine, December 19, 2017. https://www.forbes.com/sites/marissaperetz/2017/12/19/these-companies-prove-you-can-be-socially-conscious-and-profitable/#109c648a3b10.

Schoenberg, Tom. "Walmart Deadlocked With U.S. Over Bribery Probe." Bloomberg.com. Bloomberg, August 2, 2018. https://www.bloomberg.com/news/articles/2018-08-02/walmart-is-said-to-be-deadlocked-with-u-s-over-bribery-probe.

Schubert, Siri, and T. Christian Miller. "At Siemens, Bribery Was Just a Line Item." The New York Times. The New York Times, December 20, 2008. https://www.nytimes.com/2008/12/21/business/worldbusiness/21siemens.html.

Schwab, Klaus, and Xavier Sala-i-Martín. "The Global Competitiveness Report 2017-2018." Insight Report. World Economic Forum, 2017. http://www3.weforum.org/docs/

GCR2017-2018/05FullReport/TheGlobalCompetitiveness-
Report2017%E2%80%932018.pdf.

"The Impact of Disasters on Agriculture and Food Security."
Food and Agriculture Organization. United Nations, 2015.
http://www.fao.org/3/a-i5128e.pdf.

"UNHCR Policy Paper: Climate Change, Natural Disasters and Human Displacement: a UNHCR Perspective."
UNHCR. United Nations. Accessed February 10, 2018.
https://www.unhcr.org/4901e81a4.html.

Vandenbergh, Michael. "Why Private 'Actors' Are Taking
Center Stage on Climate Change." GreenBiz. GreenBiz
Group Inc., December 9, 2017. https://www.greenbiz.com/
article/why-private-actors-are-taking-center-stage-cli-
mate-change.

Venkatesan, Ravi, and Leslie Benton. "How Companies Can
Take a Stand Against Bribery." Harvard Business Review.
Harvard University, September 17, 2018. https://hbr.
org/2018/09/how-companies-can-take-a-stand-against-
bribery..

CHAPTER 5

"17 Align With Transparency Pledge; Others Should Catch Up." More Brands Should Reveal Where Their Clothes are Made. Human Rights Watch, April 20, 2017. https://www.hrw.org/news/2017/04/20/more-brands-should-reveal-where-their-clothes-are-made.

Chouinard, Yvon, and Brendan Leonard. "17 Great Yvon Chouinard Quotes." Essays. Adventure Journal, November 11, 2014. https://www.adventure-journal.com/2014/11/the-aj-list-17-great-yvon-chouinard-quotes/.

"Fiscal Year 2017." Annual Benefit Corporation Report 2017. Patagonia, 2018. https://www.patagonia.com/static/on/demandware.static/-/Library-Sites-PatagoniaShared/default/dw824facof/PDF-US/2017-BCORP-pages_022218.pdf.

Kashyap, Aruna. "When Clothing Labels Are a Matter of Life or Death." Human Rights Watch Women's Rights Division. The Daily Beast, May 2, 2018. https://www.hrw.org/news/2018/05/02/when-clothing-labels-are-matter-life-or-death.

Meltzer, Marisa. "Patagonia and The North Face: Saving the World – One Puffer Jacket at a Time." The Guardian. Guardian News and Media, March 7, 2017. https://www.

theguardian.com/business/2017/mar/07/the-north-face-patagonia-saving-world-one-puffer-jacket-at-a-time.

"Our DWR Problem [Updated]." The Cleanest Line. Patagonia, September 8, 2015. http://www.patagonia.com/blog/2015/09/our-dwr-problem-updated/.

CHAPTER 6

"Bank of America and IEEW: Investing in Women Leaders from Afghanistan and Rwanda." About Bank of America. Bank of America, May 6, 2016. https://about.bankofamerica.com/en-us/partnering-locally/boa-ieew-partnership.html#fbid=arR-cEe6X85.

Barbaro, Michael, and Coral Davenport. "Aims of Donor Are Shadowed by Past in Coal." The New York Times. The New York Times, July 4, 2014. https://www.nytimes.com/2014/07/05/us/politics/prominent-environmentalist-helped-fund-coal-projects.html.

Bennett, Amy. "The Economics of Sustainable and Impact Investing." Real Leaders. Real Leaders, May 7, 2018. https://real-leaders.com/the-economics-of-sustainable-and-impact-investing/.

Chort, Valerie, and Hamoon Ekhtiari. "A New Model for CSR (SSIR)." Stanford Social Innovation Review. Stanford University, 2018. https://ssir.org/articles/entry/a_new_model_for_csr.

"Cramer's 'Mad Money' Recap: Sin Stocks." TheStreet. TheStreet, August 30, 2006. https://www.thestreet.com/story/10306493/1/cramers-mad-money-recap-sin-stocks.html.

Daly, John. "Vice Fund Tempted by More than Tobacco and Booze." Irish Examiner. Irishexaminer.com, August 7, 2018. https://www.irishexaminer.com/breakingnews/business/vice-fund-tempted-by-more-than-tobacco-and-booze-860446.html.

Friede, Gunnar, Timo Busch, and Alexander Bassen. "ESG and Financial Performance: Aggregated Evidence from More than 2000 Empirical Studies." Journal of Sustainable Finance and Investment. Deutsche Bank Asset Management and University of Hamburg, January 14, 2016. https://www.db.com/newsroom_news/2016/ghp/esg-and-financial-performance-aggregated-evidence-from-more-than-200-empirical-studies-en-11363.htm.

Fullerton, John. "Six Reasons Why Our Stock Markets Are No Longer Fit for Purpose." The Guardian. Guardian News and Media, October 21, 2013. https://www.theguardian.com/sustainable-business/stock-markets-no-longer-fit-purpose.

Gurdus, Lizy. "Paul Tudor Jones: The $19 Trillion Private Sector Should Lead Social Change." CNBC. CNBC, November 2, 2018. https://www.cnbc.com/2018/11/02/paul-tudor-jones-the-private-sector-can-lead-social-change.html.

"Hefner's Playboy Buyout Seen Closing Friday As Tender Minimum Met." Dow Jones Newswire. Wall Street Journal, March 4, 2011. http://online.wsj.com/article/BT-CO-20110304-708619.html.

Hickel, Jason. "The Microfinance Delusion: Who Really Wins?" The Guardian. Guardian News and Media, June 10, 2015. https://www.theguardian.com/global-development-professionals-network/2015/jun/10/the-microfinance-delusion-who-really-wins.

"Hugh Hefner Sells LA Property as Financial Crisis Hits Playboy." The Telegraph. Telegraph Media Group, August 11, 2009. https://www.telegraph.co.uk/finance/recession/6007514/Hugh-Hefner-sells-LA-property-as-finan-cial-crisis-hits-Playboy.html.

Hulme, David, Joseph Hanlon, and Armando Barrientos. "Just Give Money to the Poor: The Development Revolution from the Global South." Kumarian Press, 2012. https://books.google.co.za/books/about/Just_Give_Money_to_the_Poor.html?id=M2WWHIzQONoC&hl=en.

Jimenez, Guillermo, and Elizabeth Pulos. 2014. "Corruption In International Business". *Good Corporation, Bad Corporation: Corporate Social Responsibility In The Global Economy.* https://milnepublishing.geneseo.edu/good-corporation-bad-corporation/chapter/10-corruption-in-international-business/.

Lund, Brian. "Why Even the Righteous Should Invest in Sin." AOL.com. AOL, September 19, 2014. https://www.aol.com/article/finance/2014/09/19/sin-stocks-good-investments/20962595/.

"Report on US Sustainable, Responsible, and Impact Investing Trends 2014." The Forum for Responsible and Sustainable Investment. USSIF Foundation and Bloomberg, 2014. https://www.ussif.org/Files/Publications/SIF_Trends_14.F.ES.pdf.

Vermaelen, Theo. "Doing Good by Investing in Sin." INSEAD Knowledge. Institut Européen d'Administration des Affaires, June 30, 2016. https://knowledge.insead.edu/blog/insead-blog/doing-good-by-investing-in-sin-4774.

CHAPTER 7

Autor, David H. "Why Are There Still So Many Jobs? The History and Future of Workplace Automation." economics. mit.edu. Journal of Economic Perspectives, 2015. https://economics.mit.edu/files/11563.

Bain, Marc. "Hands Required: One Very Basic Job in Sneaker Manufacturing Is Testing the Limits of Automation." Quartz. Quartz, April 24, 2017. https://qz.com/966882/robots-cant-lace-shoes-so-sneaker-production-cant-be-fully-automated-just-yet/.

"Democracy Is Good for Business." Freedom at Issue Blog. Freedom House, August 3, 2015. https://freedomhouse.org/blog/democracy-good-business.

Donovan, John, and Cathy Benko. "Inside AT&T's Radical Talent Overhaul." Harvard Business Review. Harvard University, October 7, 2016. https://hbr.org/2016/10/atts-talent-overhaul.

Easterly, William. "The Middle Class Consensus and Economic Development." williameasterly.files.wordpress.com. World Bank Group, August 2010. https://williameasterly.files.wordpress.com/2010/08/34_easterly_middleclassconsensus_prp.pdf.

Elliott, Larry. "Robots Will Take Our Jobs. We'd Better Plan Now, before It's Too Late | Larry Elliott." The Guardian. Guardian News and Media, February 1, 2018. https://www.theguardian.com/commentisfree/2018/feb/01/robots-take-our-jobs-amazon-go-seattle.

"Employment in Industry (% of Total Employment) (Modeled ILO Estimate)." The World Bank. International Labor Organization, ILOSTAT database, 2017. https://data.worldbank.org/indicator/SL.IND.EMPL.ZS?contextual=default&end=2017&locations=TH-KH-VN-LA-ID-PH-MM-TL-1W&start=1991&view=chart.

"Employment in Industry (% of Total Employment) (Modeled ILO Estimate)." World Bank. International Labor Organization, ILOSTAT database, 2017. https://data.worldbank.org/indicator/SL.IND.EMPL.ZS?contextual=default&end=2017&locations=BN-MY-SG&start=1991&type=points&view=chart.

"Employment in Industry (% of Total Employment) (Modeled ILO Estimate)." World Bank. International Labor Organization, ILOSTAT database, 2017. https://data. worldbank.org/indicator/SL.IND.EMPL.ZS?contextual=default&end=2017&locations=TH-KH-VN-LA-ID-PH-MM-TL&start=1991&view=chart.

Firth, Niall. "This Time Robots Really Are Going to Take Our Jobs." Slate Magazine. Slate, May 4, 2014. https://slate.com/technology/2014/05/robots-taking-jobs-technology-will-replace-driving-routine-physical-labor-information-processing.html.

Gavett, Gretchen. "How Self-Service Kiosks Are Changing Customer Behavior." Harvard Business Review. Harvard University, March 11, 2015. https://hbr.org/2015/03/how-self-service-kiosks-are-changing-customer-behavior.

"Global Science and Digital Skills Partnerships." Our Partners. Microsoft. Accessed December 29, 2018. https://www.microsoft.com/en-us/digital-skills/partners.

Goldfarb, Avi, Ryan C. McDevitt, Sampsa Samila, and Brian Silverman. "The E-Ect of Social Interaction on Economic Transactions: Evidence from Changes in Two Retail Formats." rotman.utoronto.ca. University of Toronto Rotman

School of Management, June 2014. http://www-2.rotman. utoronto.ca/~agoldfarb/socialtransactions.pdf.

Grace, Christine LaFave. "Help (Still) Wanted: Manufacturers Struggle to Fill Open Jobs." Plant Services. Putman Media, June 14, 2018. https://www.plantservices.com/articles/2018/wf-help-still-wanted-manufacturers-struggle-to-fill-open-jobs/?show=all.

"Greater Lawrence Regional Vocational Technical School." Massachusetts School and District Profiles. Massachusetts Department of Elementary and Secondary Education. Accessed December 27, 2018. http://profiles. doe.mass.edu/general/general.aspx?topNavID=1&left-NavId=100&orgcode=08230000&orgtypecode=5.

"Human-Robot Collaboration (HRC)." kuka.com. KUKA. Accessed December 28, 2018. https://www.kuka.com/ nb-no/technologies/human-robot-collaboration.

Inglehart, Ronald, and Christian Welzel. "How Development Leads to Democracy: What We Know About Modernization." Foreign Affairs. Foreign Affairs Magazine, 2009. https://www.foreignaffairs.com/articles/2009-03-01/ how-development-leads-democracy.

Laudicina, Paul A., Courtney Rickert McCaffrey, and Erik R. Peterson. "Rising to the Challenge: 2018 Views from the C-Suite." An Annual Survey of Global Business Executives. A. T. Kearney Global Business Policy Council, 2018. https://www.atkearney.com/web/global-business-policy-council/views-from-the-c-suite/.

Lee, Timothy B. "27 Charts That Will Change How You Think about the American Economy." Vox. Vox, October 10, 2016. https://www.vox.com/new-money/2016/10/10/12933426/27-charts-changing-economy.

Marche, Stephen. "Everybody Knows Robots Will Take Our Jobs, But We Can't Admit It. Why?" Esquire. Esquire, October 11, 2017. https://www.esquire.com/news-politics/news/a42876/millennial-financial-crisis-technology/.

Maze, Jonathan. "Kiosks Are No Labor Savior." On the Margin. Nation's Restaurant News, June 26, 2017. https://www.nrn.com/operations/kiosks-are-no-labor-savior.

McDonald, Clare. "Cisco Aims to Upskill 250,000 People by 2020." ComputerWeekly.com. Computer Weekly, October 24, 2017. https://www.computerweekly.com/news/450428800/Cisco-aims-to-upskill-250000-people-by-2020.

McIntosh, Steve. "Hollowing out and the Future of the Labour Market." www.gov.uk/bis. United Kingdom Department for Business, Innovation and Skills, October 2013. https://assets.publishing.service.gov.uk/government/uploads/system/uploads/attachment_data/file/250206/bis-13-1213-hollowing-out-and-future-of-the-labour-market.pdf.

Morgan, Blake. "Robots Will Take Our Jobs And We Need A Plan: 4 Scenarios For The Future." Forbes. Forbes Magazine, September 7, 2018. https://www.forbes.com/sites/blakemorgan/2018/09/05/robots-will-take-our-jobs-and-we-need-a-plan-4-scenarios-for-the-future/.

Moyo, Dambisa. "Why the Survival of Democracy Depends on a Strong Middle-Class." The Globe and Mail. The Globe and Mail, Inc., April 20, 2018. https://www.theglobeandmail.com/opinion/article-why-the-survival-of-democracy-depends-on-a-strong-middle-class/.

"Panera Bread (PNRA) Ronald M. Shaich on Q2 2015 Results - Earnings Call Transcript." Seeking Alpha. Panera Bread, July 29, 2015. https://seekingalpha.com/article/3370365-panera-bread-pnra-ronald-m-shaich-on-q2-2015-results-earnings-call-transcript?part=single.

Pomranz, Mike. "Self-Serve Kiosks May Not Be Killing Fast Food Jobs After All." Food & Wine, June 26, 2017. https://

www.foodandwine.com/news/self-serve-kiosks-may-not-be-killing-fast-food-jobs-after-all.

Ramaswamy, K. V. "Technological Change, Automation and Employment: A Short Review of Theory and Evidence." www.igidr.ac.in. Indira Gandhi Institute of Development Research, Mumbai, January 2018. http://www.igidr.ac.in/pdf/publication/WP-2018-002.pdf.

Rensi, Ed. "McDonald's Says Goodbye Cashiers, Hello Kiosks." Forbes. Forbes Magazine, July 11, 2018. https://www.forbes.com/sites/edrensi/2018/07/11/mcdonalds-says-goodbye-cashiers-hello-kiosks/#3b2a786d6f14.

Rynhart, Gary. "ASEAN in Transformation: How Technology Is Changing Jobs and Enterprises." Bureau for Employers' Activities. International Labour Organization, April 17, 2017. https://www.ilo.org/wcmsp5/groups/public/---asia/---ro-bangkok/---ilo-jakarta/documents/presentation/wcms_552346.pdf.

Santos, Indhira. "Labor Market Polarization in Developing Countries: Challenges Ahead." World Bank Blogs. World Bank Group, June 10, 2016. http://blogs.worldbank.org/developmenttalk/labor-market-polarization-developing-countries-challenges-ahead.

Schwartz, Jeff, Laurence Collins, Heather Stockton, Darryl Wagner, and Brett Walsh. "The Future of Work: The Augmented Workforce." 2017 Global Human Capital Trends. Deloitte Insights, February 28, 2017. https://www2.deloitte.com/insights/us/en/focus/human-capital-trends/2017/future-workforce-changing-nature-of-work.html.

Scroxton, Alex. "Automation and CSR Are Driving Reskilling Process for UK Plc, Says Cisco." ComputerWeekly.com, November 6, 2018. https://www.computerweekly.com/news/252452041/Automation-and-CSR-are-driving-reskilling-process-for-UK-plc-says-Cisco.

Scroxton, Alex. "Automation and CSR Are Driving Reskilling Process for UK Plc, Says Cisco." ComputerWeekly.com. Computer Weekly, November 6, 2016. https://www.computerweekly.com/news/252452041/Automation-and-CSR-are-driving-reskilling-process-for-UK-plc-says-Cisco.

"The Juntos Shoe: Look Good. Do Good." juntosproject.com. Juntos Project. Accessed December 29, 2018. http://www.juntosproject.com/#purposeHeaderContainer.

"Total U.S. Population." World Bank Group. United Nations Population Division, 2016. https://data.worldbank.org/indicator/SP.POP.TOTL?end=2016&locations=US&start=1965.

Vargas, Susan. "Robots in the Workplace." Safety+Health
Magazine. National Safety Council Congress and Expo,
March 25, 2018. https://www.safetyandhealthmagazine.
com/articles/16789-robots-in-the-workplace.

Varrasi, John. "Transforming the Textile Industry." ASME.
org. The American Society of Mechanical Engineers,
April 2012. https://www.asme.org/engineering-topics/arti-
cles/manufacturing-processing/transforming-the-tex-
tile-industry.

Wike, Richard, and Bruce Stokes. "In Advanced and Emerging Economies Alike, Worries About Job Automation."
Pew Research Center's Global Attitudes Project. Pew
Research Center's Global Attitudes Project, September 20, 2018. http://www.pewglobal.org/2018/09/13/
in-advanced-and-emerging-economies-alike-wor-
ries-about-job-automation/.

CHAPTER 8

"2014 McDonald's Sustainability Report." The Good Business
Report. McDonald's, 2014. https://corporate.mcdonalds.
com/content/dam/gwscorp/scale-for-good/2014_sustain-
ability_report.pdf.

"Accenture Reports Very Strong Fourth-Quarter and Full-Year Fiscal 2015 Results." newsroom.accenture.com. Accenture, September 24, 2015. https://newsroom.accenture.com/news/accenture-reports-very-strong-fourth-quarter-and-full-year-fiscal-2015-results.htm.

Alhouti, Sarah, Catherine M. Johnson, and Betsey Bugg Holloway. "Corporate Social Responsibility Authenticity: Investigating Its Antecedents and Outcomes." Journal of Business Research. Elsevier, March 2016. https://www.sciencedirect.com/science/article/pii/S0148296315004063.

Churchill, Winston. "The Worst Form of Government." The International Churchill Society. The International Churchill Society, March 20, 2017. https://winstonchurchill.org/resources/quotes/the-worst-form-of-government/.

Fullerton, Jamie. "Suicide at Chinese IPhone Factory Reignites Concern over Working Conditions." The Telegraph. Telegraph Media Group, January 7, 2018. https://www.telegraph.co.uk/news/2018/01/07/suicide-chinese-iphone-factory-reignites-concern-working-conditions/.

Harris, Jennifer L., Marlene B. Scwartz, and Kelly D. Brownell. "Fast Food Advertising to Children and Teens Score." fastfoodmarketing.org. Yale Rudd Center for Food

Policy and Obesity, 2010. http://fastfoodmarketing.org/
media/FastFoodFACTS_Report_Summary_2010.pdf.

Khanna, Parag, and David Francis. "These 25 Companies Are
More Powerful Than Many Countries." Foreign Policy.
Foreign Policy, 2016. https://foreignpolicy.com/2016/03/15/
these-25-companies-are-more-powerful-than-ma-
ny-countries-multinational-corporate-wealth-power/.

Knudsen, Jette Steen. "Government Regulation of Corporate
Social Responsibility (CSR): Implications for Corporate
Governance." Edited by Ciaran Driver and Grahame
Thompson. Social Science Research Network.
Oxford University Press, September 19, 2017.
https://poseidon01.ssrn.com/delivery.php?ID=73601
3002124027103100076013018107006049071000
8034054034076086125076112022014102104011 0
2803902811905202205107709809500108007
1007040038068062019124100083102070 02
41070050140360801160931250910230171000
8911711600610012411901807308600931231150
68067089123118078&EXT=pdf.

Landrum, Sarah. "Millennials Driving Brands
To Practice Socially Responsible Marketing."
Forbes. Forbes Magazine, March 17, 2017. https://
www.forbes.com/sites/sarahlandrum/2017/03/17/

millennials-driving-brands-to-practice-socially-responsi-
ble-marketing/#56eb1a0d4990.

Lappe, Anna. "Lifestyle." blueocean.net. Blue Ocean Network. Accessed February 24, 2019. https://blueocean.net/
lifestyle/page/10/.

Mohr, Lois A., Deborah J. Webb, and Katherine E. Harris.
"Do Consumers Expect Companies to Be Socially Responsible? The Impact of Corporate Social Responsibility on Buying Behavior." JSTOR. The Journal of Consumer Affairs,
2001. https://www-jstor-org.proxy.library.georgetown.edu/
stable/23860071?seq=23#metadata_info_tab_contents.

Tuttle, Brad. "McDonald's Sales Rise with Focus on Core
Menu, Not Health | Money." Everyday Money. Meredith
Corporation, April 22, 2016. http://time.com/money/4303546/
mcdonalds-big-mac-fries-health/.